READINGS ON

OTHELLO

THE GREENHAVEN PRESS
Literary Companion
TO BRITISH LITERATURE

READINGS ON

OTHELLO

Don Nardo, *Book Editor*

David L. Bender, *Publisher*
Bruno Leone, *Executive Editor*
Bonnie Szumski, *Series Editor*

Greenhaven Press, Inc., San Diego, CA

Library of Congress Cataloging-in-Publication Data

Readings on Othello / Don Nardo, book editor.
     p.   cm. — (The Greenhaven Press literary companion to British literature)
    Includes bibliographical references and index.
    ISBN 0-7377-0187-0 (lib. bdg. : alk. paper). — ISBN 0-7377-0186-2 (pbk. : alk. paper)
    1. Shakespeare, William, 1564–1616. Othello. 2. Muslims in literature. 3. Blacks in literature. 4. Tragedy. I. Nardo, Don. II. Series.
PR2829.R38 2000
822.3'3—dc21
                                 99-29219
                                    CIP

Cover photo: Archive Photos

Copyright © 2000 by Greenhaven Press, Inc.
PO Box 289009
San Diego, CA 92198-9009
Printed in the U.S.A.

"O, Beware, my lord, of
jealousy!
It is the green-eyed monster,
which doth mock
The meat it feeds on. . . .
Poor and content is rich, and
rich enough;
But riches fineless is as poor as
winter
To him that ever fears he shall
be poor.
Good God the souls of all my
tribe defend
From jealousy! **"**

Iago to Othello, act 3, scene 3

CONTENTS

Chapter 1: The Plot, Setting, Language, and Imagery of *Othello*

1. The Story of *Othello*
by Charles and Mary Lamb   30

The story of Othello, the Moorish general whose life is destroyed by jealousy and betrayal, is one of the most compelling in English literature. This overview of the plot of Shakespeare's play *Othello*, written by a renowned nineteenth-century scholar and his sister, not only covers the main events of the story, but also captures the mood of the scenes and style of the language.

2. Local Color and Other Elements of Setting in *Othello* by John W. Draper   41

The two major settings of the play are the colorful and stately Italian city of Venice and the exotic, faraway Mediterranean island of Cyprus. Shakespeare also briefly mentions places and customs of another Italian city— Florence—as well as Moorish North Africa, presumably Othello's birthplace.

3. Shakespeare's Use of Language Defines the Play's Main Characters *by Norman Sanders*   52

In *Othello,* Shakespeare skillfully uses language not only to create atmosphere but also to give the characters personality, color, and depth. For instance, Iago employs a crude, often repulsive vocabulary, reflecting his lack of imagination and mean-spirited nature; while Othello's romantic, pleasingly poetic speeches reveal his heroic, noble nature.

4. Musical Images and References Unite the Play's Scenes and Ideas *by Ros King*   61

As Othello, poisoned by Iago's lies, grows distant from Desdemona, she remarks that her life and marriage are "not now in tune," one of the numerous musical images (along

with the singing of songs and the playing of instruments)
that help to give the play thematic and structural unity.

Chapter 2: The Play's Pivotal Characters

here by a renowned scholar, are Brabantio, her father; Cassio, the young man whom Iago claims is her lover; and Roderigo, her former suitor, who still carries a torch for her.

Chapter 3: Central Themes and Ideas Developed in *Othello*

Chapter 4: Major Modern Stage and Film Adaptations of the Play

FOREWORD

*"'Tis the good reader that
makes the good book."*

Ralph Waldo Emerson

The story's bare facts are simple: The captain, an old and scarred seafarer, walks with a peg leg made of whale ivory. He relentlessly drives his crew to hunt the world's oceans for the great white whale that crippled him. After a long search, the ship encounters the whale and a fierce battle ensues. Finally the captain drives his harpoon into the whale, but the harpoon line catches the captain about the neck and drags him to his death.

A simple story, a straightforward plot—yet, since the 1851 publication of Herman Melville's *Moby-Dick*, readers and critics have found many meanings in the struggle between Captain Ahab and the whale. To some, the novel is a cautionary tale that depicts how Ahab's obsession with revenge leads to his insanity and death. Others believe that the whale represents the unknowable secrets of the universe and that Ahab is a tragic hero who dares to challenge fate by attempting to discover this knowledge. Perhaps Melville intended Ahab as a criticism of Americans' tendency to become involved in well-intentioned but irrational causes. Or did Melville model Ahab after himself, letting his fictional character express his anger at what he perceived as a cruel and distant god?

Although literary critics disagree over the meaning of *Moby-Dick*, readers do not need to choose one particular interpretation in order to gain an understanding of Melville's novel. Instead, by examining various analyses, they can gain numerous insights into the issues that lie under the surface of the basic plot. Studying the writings of literary critics can also aid readers in making their own assessments of *Moby-Dick* and other literary works and in developing analytical thinking skills.

The Greenhaven Literary Companion Series was created with these goals in mind. Designed for young adults, this unique anthology series provides an engaging and comprehensive introduction to literary analysis and criticism. The essays included in the Literary Companion Series are chosen for their accessibility to a young adult audience and are expertly edited in consideration of both the reading and comprehension levels of this audience. In addition, each essay is introduced by a concise summation that presents the contributing writer's main themes and insights. Every anthology in the Literary Companion Series contains a varied selection of critical essays that cover a wide time span and express diverse views. Wherever possible, primary sources are represented through excerpts from authors' notebooks, letters, and journals and through contemporary criticism.

Each title in the Literary Companion Series pays careful consideration to the historical context of the particular author or literary work. In-depth biographies and detailed chronologies reveal important aspects of authors' lives and emphasize the historical events and social milieu that influenced their writings. To facilitate further research, every anthology includes primary and secondary source bibliographies of articles and/or books selected for their suitability for young adults. These engaging features make the Greenhaven Literary Companion series ideal for introducing students to literary analysis in the classroom or as a library resource for young adults researching the world's great authors and literature.

Exceptional in its focus on young adults, the Greenhaven Literary Companion Series strives to present literary criticism in a compelling and accessible format. Every title in the series is intended to spark readers' interest in leading American and world authors, to help them broaden their understanding of literature, and to encourage them to formulate their own analyses of the literary works that they read. It is the editors' hope that young adult readers will find these anthologies to be true companions in their study of literature.

INTRODUCTION

One day in the early 1960s, the late noted English drama critic and theatrical manager Kenneth Tynan and the late Laurence Olivier, now widely regarded as the greatest English-speaking actor of the twentieth century, were discussing the upcoming agenda of England's recently established National Theater. Tynan urged Olivier to play Othello, the only major Shakespearean tragic role the actor had not yet attempted. (Olivier had previously played Romeo, Hamlet, Macbeth, and King Lear, most of these more than once.) To this suggestion, Olivier delivered the following often-quoted reply:

> I think Shakespeare and Richard Burbage [the playwright's friend and the most renowned tragedian of the Elizabethan stage] got drunk together one night and Burbage said, "I can play anything you write, anything at all." And Shakespeare said, "Right, I'll fix you, boy!" And then he wrote *Othello*." [1]

Olivier went on to call the role of Othello a "monstrous, monstrous burden" for any actor. [2] He was in part acknowledging the tremendous emotional demands of the role, that of a Moorish general whose officer and close associate, Iago, convinces him that his wife, Desdemona, is having an affair with another man; the charge is false, but the trusting Othello believes it and, inflamed with jealousy, goes on to kill the unfortunate Desdemona. Olivier also worried about the way Shakespeare wrote the character of Othello's nemesis. A classic dastardly villain, the crafty, scheming Iago had been known to "steal the thunder" (overshadow) the unknowing and gullible Othello in many a stage production of the play, and Olivier did not relish being upstaged by other actors. (Eventually, the challenge of attacking so great a part overcame these worries. Olivier played Othello on both stage and screen and his magnificent performance has become legendary.)

One thing that neither Olivier nor other renowned actors and directors who have tackled (and continue to tackle)

Othello over the years doubted for a moment was the play's power to attract and entertain modern audiences. Though written some four hundred years ago, the play remains, and perhaps will always remain, both relevant and riveting. This is mainly because it examines, in a realistic and often disturbing manner, primal human emotions that all audience members recognize, relate to, or have experienced firsthand, chiefly love, hatred, pride, and especially jealousy and betrayal. Moreover, the plot unfolds swiftly, with almost no wasted words or moments; all the while suspense builds as the audience hopes anxiously that the title character will come to his senses, see that Iago is a liar, and spare the innocent Desdemona. The late, highly regarded Shakespearean scholar A.C. Bradley summed up the play's appeal this way:

> Of all Shakespeare's tragedies . . . *Othello* is the most painfully exciting and the most terrible. From the moment when the temptation of the hero begins, the reader's heart and mind are held in a vice, experiencing the extremes of pity and fear, sympathy and repulsion, sickening hope and dreadful expectation. . . . In the second place, there is no subject more exciting than sexual jealousy rising to the pitch of passion; and there can hardly be any spectacle at once so engrossing and so painful as that of a great nature suffering the torment of this passion, and driven by it to a crime which is also a hideous blunder.[5]

Add to *Othello*'s emotional power, relevance to all times and places, and deft, economical construction its colorful setting (medieval Venice and Cyprus) and beautiful language; the result is a successful recipe for continued widespread interest in reading, studying, staging, and viewing the play.

The essays selected for the Greenhaven Literary Companion to Shakespeare's *Othello* provide teachers and students with a wide range of information and opinion about the play and its author's style, themes, and outlook on the human condition. All of the authors of the essays are or were (until their deaths) noted professors at leading colleges and universities, scholars specializing in Shakespearean studies, and/or noted stage and film critics. Among this companion volume's several special features: Each essay explains or discusses in detail a specific, narrowly focused topic; the introduction to each essay previews the main points; and inserts interspersed within the essays serve as examples of ideas expressed by the authors, offer supplementary information, or add authenticity and color. These inserts come from *Othello,* from critical commentary about the play, or from other scholarly sources. Above all, this companion book is designed to increase the reader's understanding and enjoyment of one of the most popular and often-performed plays in the theatrical canon.

NOTES

1. Quoted in Anthony Holden, *Laurence Olivier: A Biography*. New York: Atheneum, 1988, p. 376.
2. Quoted in Holden, *Laurence Olivier*, p. 376.
3. A.C. Bradley, *Shakespearean Tragedy*. 1956. Reprint, New York: Viking Penguin, 1991, pp. 177–78.

WILLIAM SHAKESPEARE AND OTHELLO, THE MOOR OF VENICE

Othello is not only one of Shakespeare's most skillfully written plays but also one of the most powerful and controversial plays ever written, a work that is almost guaranteed to evoke strong reactions from audiences of all ages and nationalities. In the words of literary editor Julie Hankey, the play

> has laid hold of people, primitively, in a way that no other Shakespearean tragedy could hope to do. Women have shrieked and fainted, old men have laid their heads down on their arms and sobbed, young men have lost their sleep and gone about for days in a trance.

One important reason for such reactions, Hankey continues, is that "the story comes very near to ordinary people's lives."[1]

Indeed, this tale about a proud military man (Othello) whose officer and supposed friend (Iago) dupes him into believing that his wife (Desdemona) has betrayed him and killing her for it is laden with emotionally charged elements and issues. First, there is Iago's real betrayal of his friend, juxtaposed with the pitiful image of an innocent young woman wrongly accused of the same hurtful act. In addition, the audience is pummeled by Iago's explicit and lurid descriptions of Desdemona's supposed sexual exploits; Othello's explosive outbursts of jealousy and rage at hearing about them; confrontations between Othello and his wife in which he physically as well as verbally abuses her; and the terrible and graphic sight of the title character smothering a young woman whom the audience knows conclusively is innocent.

As if all of this were not powerful enough, racial overtones intensify the drama. Othello is black (or at least dark-skinned; actors have played him in a range of colors and ethnic backgrounds); Desdemona is white. The words of Iago's wife, Emilia, on discovering Desdemona's body—"O, the more angel she, and you the blacker devil,"—have echoed and inflamed the deep-seated prejudices of a great many spectators over the

15

centuries.[2] Indeed, only in recent decades have American audiences tolerated the sight of a black man kissing, striking, and killing a white woman. In 1930, when the United States was still a deeply racist society, a major tour of the play starring the black actor Paul Robeson was canceled because of fear of violent audience reaction. (A revival of the production opened to critical acclaim on Broadway in 1943.) In fact, the play already had a history of inciting violent outbursts. In a nineteenth-century production staged in the American West, for instance, a spectator thought Iago so despicable that he took out a pistol and shot him to death.[3]

That *Othello* continues to elicit strong audience reaction is remarkable when one considers that the play has been known for centuries (during which it has been staged thousands of times in many different languages) and that most spectators already know the basics of its plot and ending before the curtain rises. It is likely that its author fully intended it to be powerful and controversial, including in its racial overtones, even in his own day, for his main aim was to draw and maintain the interest of large audiences, and many Elizabethan spectators undoubtedly disapproved of racially mixed marriages. Yet there is every indication that, whatever his white audiences may have thought of the black title character, Shakespeare himself saw Othello as an exceptionally good and noble individual. "Only those who have not read the play at all," remark noted scholars Alice Walker and John D. Wilson,

> could suppose that Shakespeare shared the prejudice, insomuch as Othello is his noblest soldier and he obviously exerted himself to represent him as a spirit of the rarest quality. . . . Before such dignity, self-possession and serene sense of power, racial prejudice dwindles to a petty stupidity; and when Othello has told the lovely story of his courtship, and Desdemona has . . . simply and without a moment's hesitation, preferred her black husband to her white father, we have to admit that the union of these two grand persons, so far from being unnatural, is that rare human event, the marriage of true minds and a real love-match.[4]

A WELL-DOCUMENTED LIFE IN A DYNAMIC AGE

That Shakespeare had the tolerance and personal insight to see and expound on the qualities of people whose races, societies, and beliefs were very different from his own is surely due in large part to his expansive intellect and broad (though mostly informal) education. The exact details of his life, especially his early years, are unknown. Yet the often voiced notion that the

great playwright led an almost totally mysterious and undocumented life (which has given rise to numerous vain attempts to
prove that someone else wrote his plays) is a misconception.
The fact is that for a common person of the Elizabethan period
(spanning the late 1500s and early 1600s) Shakespeare's life
was unusually *well* documented. The evidence consists of
more than a hundred official documents, including entries
about him and his relatives in parish registers and town
archives, legal records involving property transfers, and business letters to or about him. There are also more than fifty allusions to him and his works in the published writings of his
contemporaries. These sources do not tell us much about
Shakespeare's personality, likes and dislikes, and personal beliefs. Yet they provide enough information to piece together a
concise outline of the important events of his life.

Shakespeare was born in Stratford, now called Stratford-
on-Avon, a village in Warwickshire in central England, in
1564. The exact date is somewhat uncertain but tradition accepts it as April 23. If this dating is indeed correct, it is an unusual coincidence, for April 23 is celebrated in England as St.
George's Day, in honor of the country's patron saint, and is
also the documented month and day of Shakespeare's own
death fifty-two years later.[5]

Much more important is the fact that Shakespeare came
into the world at a pivotal time in history—the last decades of
the sixteenth century—and in what was then one of the
world's most important nations—England. As it happened,
this was one of the richest, most dynamic, and most oppor-
tune cultural and professional settings for aspiring poets and
dramatists in all of Western history. Many great writers,
among them Francis Bacon, Christopher Marlowe, Ben Jonson, and John Donne, were all born within a dozen years of
Shakespeare's birth and published works during his lifetime.
Writing plays was then, for the first time in England's history,
seen as a legitimate art form, as evidenced partly by the construction of England's first public theater when Shakespeare
was twelve.

Moreover, Shakespeare was born into a time when powerful European nations like England were greatly expanding
their horizons. It was "an era of change and restlessness," remarks Shakespearean scholar Karl Holzknecht.

> Everywhere—in religion, in philosophy, in politics, in science, in
> literature—new ideas were springing into life and coming into
> conflict with the established order of things. . . . A whole series of

events and discoveries, coming together at the end of the fifteenth century [just preceding the Elizabethan age], transformed . . . many of the institutions and the habits of mind that we call medieval. The gradual break-up of feudalism . . . the discovery of gunpowder and . . . the mariner's compass and the possibility of safely navigating the limitless ocean, the production of paper and the invention of printing, and . . . the Copernican system of astronomy which formulated a new center of the universe—all of these new conceptions had a profound effect upon human thought and became the foundations for intellectual, moral, social, and economic changes which quickly made themselves felt.[6]

In addition to these forces shaping Europe in the 1500s, several important events occurred in England during Shakespeare's own lifetime. Perhaps the most renowned of these—the English defeat of the huge Spanish Armada (an event that saved England from invasion and foreign occupation)—occurred in 1588. Not long afterward, Sir Francis Drake, Sir John Hawkins, and other adventurous English sea captains helped turn the sea-lanes into great highways for England's increasingly powerful navy. And in 1607, when Shakespeare was about forty-three, English settlers founded the colony of Jamestown in Virginia, giving England a foothold in the New World.

England's command of the waves brought commercial success and its ports and cities became bustling centers of high finance, social life, and the arts. Amid all of this, the theater, increasingly recognized as an art form, provided a fertile creative atmosphere for the efforts and innovations of ambitious young playwrights like William Shakespeare.

A VORACIOUS READER

However, it was by no means evident at first that young Will Shakespeare would turn out to be a major contributor to and shaper of this new and growing theater world. When he was born, his father, John Shakespeare, was a glover and perhaps also a wool and leather dealer in Stratford, far from bustling, cosmopolitan London, where most actors, writers, and other artists congregated and worked. The elder Shakespeare also held various local community positions, among them ale taster, town councilman, town treasurer, and eventually bailiff, or mayor. John and his wife, Mary Arden, were married shortly before the accession of Elizabeth I to the English throne in 1558; they subsequently produced eight children, of whom William was the third child and eldest son.

It is fairly certain that from age seven to about age sixteen Shakespeare attended the town grammar school. There, students studied Latin grammar and literature, including the works of the Roman writers Terence, Cicero, Virgil, and Ovid, as well as works by later European authors such as the Dutch moralist Erasmus. Following the educational customs of the day, Shakespeare and his classmates had to memorize the grammar and other information and then parrot it back when drilled by the schoolmaster. A rough idea of the process is afforded in this scene from Shakespeare's *The Merry Wives of Windsor,* in which a parson (Evans) tests the Latin knowledge of a young boy (Will, a name not likely chosen by chance):

> EVANS. What is your genitive case plural, William?
>
> WILL. Genitive case?
>
> EVANS. Ay.
>
> WILL. *Horum, harum, horum.* . . .
>
> EVANS. Show me now, William, your declension of your pronouns.
>
> WILL. Forsooth [in truth], I have forgot.
>
> EVANS. It is *qui, quae, quod:* if you forget your *qui's,* your *quae's,* and your *quod's,* you must be preeches [whipped].[7]

In addition to these formal studies, Shakespeare must have done much reading on his own time in his teens and twenties. We know this partly because his works reveal a knowledge not only of Latin, but of French and several other languages. Shakespeare was also very well versed in both ancient and recent European history and fiction, including the classic works of Italy's Boccaccio and England's Chaucer. In addition, and perhaps most importantly, Shakespeare amassed a huge body of practical knowledge about life. In fact, says Shakespearean scholar John F. Andrews:

> Judging from his plays and poems, we may infer that Shakespeare was interested in virtually every aspect of human life— in professions such as law, medicine, religion, and teaching; in everyday occupations such as farming, sheepherding, tailoring, and shopkeeping; in skills such as fishing, gardening, and cooking. Much of what Shakespeare knew about these and countless other subjects he would have acquired from books. He must have been a voracious reader. But he would have learned a great deal, also, from simply being alert to all that went on around him.[8]

By his young adulthood, therefore, Shakespeare possessed an impressive, highly rounded education, most of it self-taught.

LEARNING ON THE JOB

Informed conjecture about his childhood and education aside, the first certain fact about Shakespeare after his birth was his wedding, which his marriage license dates November 27, 1582. His bride, Anne Hathaway, was the daughter of a farmer from the nearby village of Shottery. She was eight years older than he. Local documents also identify a daughter, Susanna, christened May 26, 1583, and twins, Hamnet and Judith, christened February 26, 1585; other surviving records show that Hamnet died in 1596 at the age of eleven.

The exact reason that young Will Shakespeare chose the theater as a profession is unknown. But certain facts help us form an educated guess, among them that traveling companies of actors visited and performed at Stratford periodically. For instance, Stratford records indicate such visits from the theatrical troupes the Queen's Men and the Earl of Worcester's Men in 1568 and 1569, when Shakespeare was about five. These companies presented the most popular plays of the day on makeshift wooden stages, described here by noted scholar A.A. Mendilow:

> Before 1576, there were no permanent theaters in existence in England. . . . All stage performances for public entertainment in the larger towns before and even after 1576 were conducted on movable platforms . . . covering a curtained lower story where the actors could change their costumes; the entry from below to the upper acting area could also serve as a "hell-mouth" into which the wicked were thrown in the old religious drama. The platform was open on all four sides as a rule, and perhaps had a canopy against the rain. . . . The whole cart was on wheels and constituted a traveling theater which could be set up in market squares and open spaces. In Shakespeare's time, companies of actors still traveled in the provinces, especially when performances were forbidden in London because of an outbreak of the plague.[9]

It may well be that traveling productions like these fascinated the young Shakespeare enough to inspire his going to London to try his luck in the theater, an event that likely occurred in 1587, the year before the English victory over the Spanish Armada.

Various undocumented stories have survived about the young man's first professional job. One maintains that he tended horses outside a theater until offered the position of assistant prompter. "Another theory seems more likely," writes Shakespearean scholar François Laroque, namely that

> Shakespeare attached himself to a theatrical company—perhaps the Queen's Men, which happened to have lost one of its members in a brawl. The young Shakespeare could easily have stepped into his shoes, as experience was not required. Actors learned on the job.[10]

There is little doubt that the observant and talented Shakespeare learned more quickly than most. By 1593 he had written *Richard III, The Comedy of Errors,* and *Henry VI, Parts 1, 2,* and *3,* earning him a solid reputation as a playwright and actor in the London theater scene. At first he did not attach himself exclusively to any specific theatrical company, but worked on and off with several, including that of Richard Burbage, the finest and most acclaimed actor of the time. Burbage, four years younger than Shakespeare, became the playwright's close friend and colleague and eventually played the title roles in the original productions of some of his greatest plays, including *Hamlet, Richard III, King Lear,* and *Othello.*

During most of 1593 and 1594, London's theaters were closed because of a severe outbreak of the plague, and Shakespeare temporarily channeled his energies into writing pure poetry. Two long poems, *Venus and Adonis* and *The Rape of Lucrece,* the only works he ever published himself, were completed in this interval and dedicated to the earl of Southampton, a close friend who, some evidence suggests, lent the playwright money when he needed it. These works established Shakespeare as an accepted and respectable literary figure, whereas his plays, like those of other playwrights of the time, were viewed as popular but lowbrow entertainment rather than as legitimate literature.

A SOARING REPUTATION

It might have been one of Southampton's loans (or perhaps an outright monetary gift) that enabled Shakespeare to buy a modest share of a new theatrical company, the Lord Chamberlain's Men. Its founding in 1594 marked an important turning point in the playwright's career. Performing at all the major theaters of the day, including the Theatre, the Swan, and the Curtain (the famous Globe had not yet been built), the company thereafter provided Shakespeare with a ready creative outlet for his plays as well as a regular income. By 1603, when it became known as the King's Servants, it was performing periodically at the royal court and Shakespeare was a major shareholder in all company profits.

As a permanent member of the company, Shakespeare had the opportunity to work on a regular basis with the best English actors of the day. In addition to the great Burbage, these included Henry Condell, John Heminge, William Sly, and Will Kempe. Kempe, one of the great comic players of the Elizabethan stage, specialized in broad, slapstick comedy and physical clowning. Evidence suggests that he played the role of Peter, the bumbling servant to the Nurse in *Romeo and Juliet,* and Dogberry, the constable in *Much Ado About Nothing.* Over the years Shakespeare wrote a number of comic roles especially for Kempe, among them Costard in *Love's Labor's Lost,* Launce in *The Two Gentlemen of Verona,* and Bottom in *A Midsummer Night's Dream.*

Indeed, from 1594 on Shakespeare devoted most of his time to writing plays, turning out a large number of astonishing variety and quality between 1594 and 1601. A partial list includes the comedies *The Taming of the Shrew, The Two Gentlemen of Verona, The Merry Wives of Windsor,* and *Twelfth Night;* the histories *Richard II, Henry IV, Parts 1* and *2,* and *Henry V;* and the tragedies *Romeo and Juliet, Julius Caesar,* and *Hamlet.* Not surprisingly, the playwright's reputation soared, as evidenced by this 1598 remembrance by schoolmaster Francis Meres (died 1647), praising his talent and skills:

> The sweet witty soul of [the great ancient Roman poet] Ovid lives in mellifluous [smooth and sweet] and honey-tongued Shakespeare, witness his *Venus and Adonis,* his *Lucrece,* his . . . sonnets. . . . As [the Roman playwrights] Plautus and Seneca are accounted the best for Comedy and Tragedy among the Latins: so Shakespeare among the English is the most excellent in both kinds for the stage.[11]

In the midst of turning out so many masterpieces in these years, the playwright somehow managed to find the time for journeys back and forth to rural Stratford and the family and community obligations centered there. In 1597 he became a local burgess, or council member, by buying New Place, the largest and finest home in the town (the property included two barns and two gardens). Town records show that he later bought other property in the area, confirming that he had by now acquired more than what was then viewed as a comfortable living.

THE RENOWNED GLOBE THEATER

It is probable that a significant portion of this large income must have come from Shakespeare's one-eighth share in the profits of the new and very successful Globe Theater, which opened in 1598. He and his colleagues in the Lord Chamberlain's Men had found it difficult to renew their lease at the Theatre and had decided to build their own playhouse. In the short span of eight months they built the Globe on the south side of the Thames River and entered into a joint ownership deal with Sir Nicholas Brend, who owned the property. This marked the first known instance in theatrical history of actors' owning the theater in which they performed. It was for this theater and the specific properties of its stage that Shakespeare tailored the plays he wrote in the years that followed. Shakespearean scholar Ronald Watkins, an expert on Elizabethan theaters, provides this informative description of the Globe in its heyday:

> The [building's] octagonal frame is about 84 feet in outside diameter—hardly more than the length of a lawn-tennis court. A concentric octagon within the frame bounds the Yard, which is open to the sky. Between the two octagons the space is roofed and the building rises to three stories. Nearly five of the eight sides of the octagonal frame are occupied by galleries from which the eyes of the spectators converge upon the stage. The Yard will hold 600 standing close-packed (the groundlings); the three galleries about 1,400. . . . Intimacy [between actors and audience] is possible at the Globe because of the position of the Platform [i.e., the stage]. The middle point of the front edge is the exact center of the octagon. The actor . . . can have his audience on three sides of him. There is real distance in the depth of the stage, and an actor in the Study [or discovery space, the small area, often curtained, at the rear of the stage] will seem remote while another in front seems close at hand; this contrast in their relation to the audience is often used for dramatic purpose. The Platform is the main field of action for the players. . . . It tapers towards the front, stands probably between 4 and 5 feet from the floor of the Yard, and is protected from the groundlings by rails; the front edge is 24 feet wide, at its widest it is 41 feet; its depth from front to Study-curtain is 29 feet; and the Study itself, when open, adds a further 7 or 8 feet. Conspicuous towards the front of the Platform stand the two pillars supporting the . . . Heavens [a rooflike canopy overhanging the middle of the stage]. . . . The Tiring-house [containing dressing rooms for the actors] is the permanent background to the platform; its back is turned to the afternoon sun, so that no freaks of light and shade distract from the illusion [since the plays were presented in the afternoon]. . . . On the Platform level the . . . Study is flanked by two doors . . . the two main entries for the players.[12]

Between 1600 and 1607, the Globe's open-air Yard and Platform were the scene of the premieres of most of what are now viewed as Shakespeare's greatest tragedies: *Hamlet, Othello, King Lear, Macbeth*, and *Antony and Cleopatra*.

MONUMENTS TO HIS MEMORY

Shakespeare survived the writing of these superb and timeless works by only eight years. Apparently now secure in his fame and fortune, he seems to have spent much of his time during these years at New Place in Stratford. There, according to various entries in local records and diaries, he became increasingly involved in community and family affairs. He still wrote plays, but no longer at the rapid pace he had maintained in his youth. His last works included *Coriolanus, Pericles, The Winter's Tale, Henry VIII*, and *The Two Noble Kinsmen*, all first performed between 1608 and 1613. *Kinsmen* turned out to be his swan song. He must have become seriously ill in March 1616, for his will was executed on March 25; he died nearly a month later on April 23. The bulk of his estate went to his wife, sister, and daughters Susanna and Judith, although he also left money to some of his theater colleagues, including Richard Burbage.

A few years after Shakespeare's death, a monument to him, designed by prosperous stonemason Gheerart (or Gerard) Janssen, was erected in Stratford Church. According to University of Maryland scholar Samuel Shoenbaum:

> Janssen worked mainly in white marble, with black for the two Corinthian columns, and black touchstone for the inlaid panels. The columns support a cornice [horizontal molding] on which sit two small cherubic figures, both male; the left one, holding a spade, represents Labor; the right, with a skull and inverted torch, signifies Rest. They flank the familiar Shakespearean [coat of] arms, helm, and crest, carved in bas-relief on a square stone block. The design forms a pyramid at the apex [top] of which sits another skull. . . . Wearing a sleeveless gown over a doublet, Shakespeare stands with a quill pen in his right hand, a sheet of paper under his left, both hands resting on a cushion.[15]

Shakespeare received a greater posthumous honor in 1623 when two of his former theatrical partners, Henry Condell and John Heminge, published the so-called First Folio, a collection of the playwright's complete plays, under the title *Mr. William Shakespeare's Comedies, Histories, & Tragedies. Published According to the True Original Copies.* The exact nature of these "copies" that served as the Folio's basis remains unclear. Most scholars assume that they were various "quartos," early printed versions of the plays, which the actors often used as performance scripts. Whatever its sources, the First Folio was extremely important to posterity because it included eighteen plays that had not already been printed in quarto form and that might otherwise have been lost forever. Among them were some of the playwright's greatest works— *As You Like It, Macbeth, Antony and Cleopatra, The Tempest,* and the great political play *Julius Caesar*. These works, along with Shakespeare's other plays, have been "accorded a place in our culture above and beyond their topmost place in our literature," writes Harvard University scholar Harry Levin:

> They have been virtually canonized as humanistic scriptures, the tested residue of pragmatic [practical] wisdom, a general collection of quotable texts and usable examples. Reprinted, reedited, commented upon, and translated into most languages, they have preempted more space on the library shelves than the books of—or about—any other author. Meanwhile, they have become a staple of the school and college curricula, as well as the happiest of hunting grounds for scholars and critics.[14]

THE DATE AND SOURCES FOR *OTHELLO*

Scholars and critics have certainly found happy hunting in *Othello*, which has always been ranked as one of the playwright's greatest works. In the eighteenth century it was widely seen as *the* greatest of Shakespeare's tragedies, above even *Hamlet* and *King Lear*, and a small minority of scholars still maintain that view. *Othello*, "the third of the mature tragedies," comments noted Shakespearean scholar E.A.J. Honigmann,

> contains arguably the best plot, two of Shakespeare's most original characters [Othello and Iago], the most powerful scene in any of his plays [act 3, scene 3, in which Iago convinces Othello that Desdemona has betrayed him], and poetry second to none. We may fairly call it the most exciting of the tragedies—even the most unbearably exciting—so why not the greatest? . . . Shakespeare, at the height of his powers, exerting himself to the utmost, achieved [in *Othello*] perfect command of his material and—let us put it unaggressively— gave the world a tragedy as magnificently Shakespearean as any in the canon.[15]

When was Shakespeare, as Honigmann puts it, "at the height of his powers"; in other words, when did he write *Othello*? Until the twentieth century, most scholars dated the play to about 1603, but a majority of later experts have favored late 1601 or early 1602. It cannot be a coincidence that shortly before, from August 1600 until early in 1601, the ambassador of a Moorish leader (the king of Barbary, located along the north African coast) visited Queen Elizabeth's court. This ambassador, with the long and impressive name of Abd el-Oua-hed ben Messoud ben Mohammed Anoun, was a swarthy, olive-skinned Muslim who wore a turban and long flowing robes.[16] He was present when Shakespeare's company performed before the queen, so it is certain that the playwright saw him and likely that he actually met him. It is highly probable, therefore, that the character of Othello, set to paper soon afterward, was modeled, at least physically, on this exotic visitor.

As for the story, Shakespeare's principal source was a short story in the *Hecatommithi*, a popular work first published in 1566 by the Italian writer Giraldi Cinthio.[17] From Cinthio's story, supposedly based on a true incident, the only major character name Shakespeare borrowed was that of the hero's wife—Disdemona—which the playwright changed to Desdemona. Cinthio called his Moorish general Capitano Moro and the officer who betrays him Alfiero.

Shakespeare followed the original story fairly closely, as exemplified by some of the early lines in Cinthio's story, which summarize the situation that exists at the beginning of Shakespeare's version:

> There was once in Venice a Moor, a very gallant man, who . . . was personally valiant and had given proof in warfare of great prudence and skillful energy. . . . It happened that a virtuous Lady of wondrous beauty called Disdemona, impelled [attracted] not by female [i.e., sexual] appetite but by the Moor's good qualities, fell in love with him, and he, vanquished by the Lady's beauty and noble mind, likewise was enamored of her. So propitious was their mutual love that, although the Lady's relatives did all they could to make her take another husband, they were united in marriage and lived together in such concord and tranquility while they remained in Venice, that never a word passed between them that was not loving.[18]

The major changes Shakespeare made in Cinthio's story were in its ending, which in the source is long and drawn out. Summarizing briefly, Capitano Moro and Alfiero plot Disdemona's murder together; then, one night Moro orders his wife to investigate a noise heard in a nearby chamber; when she enters, Alfiero beats her to death with a stocking filled with sand; Moro later repents and is banished from Venice, only to be killed in exile by members of Disdemona's family; meanwhile, Alfiero commits another crime and dies while being tortured for it. Shakespeare's version, by comparison, displays a far greater sense of dramatic unity, economy, and intensity. Othello carries out the murder on his own, smothering Desdemona; in a passion of regret, he commits suicide shortly afterward; Iago, after declaring defiantly "From this time forth I never will speak word,"[19] is led away in chains to be tortured and executed.

In fact, Shakespeare's version features this economy and swiftness of of movement throughout. It also contains some of the playwright's most powerful and beautiful lines and speeches; not surprisingly, these have helped attract the greatest actors of each generation to the title role. Richard Burbage played the first Othello in the early 1600s and Thomas Betterton took on the part later in that century. They were succeeded by David Garrick and John Philip Kemble in the 1700s; Edwin Booth, Edmund Kean, and Thommaso Salvini in the 1800s; and Johnston Forbes-Robertson, Paul Robeson, Orson Welles, Laurence Olivier, and James Earl Jones in the 1900s. At least seven major film versions have been made, including those starring Welles and Olivier and the most recent one (1995), with American actor Laurence Fishburne as the Moor and English actor Kenneth Branagh as Iago.[20] There is little doubt that the play, which one scholar calls "one of the most moving spectacles of the stage,"[21] and its commanding lead roles will continue to inspire new stage and screen productions for generations to come.

NOTES

1. Quoted in Norrie Epstein, *The Friendly Shakespeare: A Thoroughly Painless Guide to the Best of the Bard.* New York: Viking Penguin, 1993, p. 379.
2. *Othello* 5.2.129–30.
3. Supposedly, the slain man's tombstone bore the epitaph "Here lies the greatest actor."
4. Alice Walker and John D. Wilson, eds., *Othello.* New York: Cambridge University Press, 1971, pp. xi–xii.
5. The date of his christening is registered as April 26, 1564. Since it was then customary to baptize an infant no later than the first Sunday or holy day following its birth, most scholars favor April 22 or 23 as Shakespeare's birth date. Regarding the end of his life, the date of his burial is known— April 25, 1616; when the burial customs of the time are considered, April 23 seems a likely date for his death.
6. Karl J. Holzknecht, *The Backgrounds of Shakespeare's Plays.* New York: American Book Company, 1950, pp. 33–34.
7. *The Merry Wives of Windsor* 4.1.57–61, 74–78.
8. John F. Andrews, "The Past Is Prologue," in Wim Coleman, ed., *Othello.* Logan, IA: Perfection Form Company, 1987, pp. viii–ix.
9. "The Elizabethan Theater," in A.A. Mendilow and Alice Shalvi, *The World and Art of Shakespeare.* New York:

Daniel Davey, 1967, pp. 26–27.

10. François Laroque, *The Age of Shakespeare.* New York: Harry N. Abrams, 1993, p. 39.

11. Quoted in "Life of Shakespeare," in Mendilow and Shalvi, *World and Art of Shakespeare,* p. 9.

12. Ronald Watkins, *On Producing Shakespeare.* New York: Benjamin Blom, 1964, pp. 18–20.

13. Samuel Schoenbaum, *William Shakespeare: A Compact Documentary Life.* New York: Oxford University Press, 1977, p. 308.

14. Harry Levin, ed., *The Riverside Shakespeare.* Boston: Houghton Mifflin, 1974, p. 1.

15. E.A.J. Honigmann, ed., *Othello.* The Arden Shakespeare. Surrey, England: Thomas Nelson and Sons, 1997, pp. 1, 111.

16. An English painting of this ambassador has survived and is on display at the Shakespeare Institute at England's University of Birmingham.

17. It is still unclear whether Shakespeare read the original Italian version or a French translation by Gabriel Chappuys. No sixteenth-century English version of Cinthio's work has survived.

18. Quoted in Honigmann, *Othello,* p. 371.

19. *Othello* 5.2.301.

20. Note also the excellent 1947 film *A Double Life,* in which actor Ronald Coleman (whose portrayal won him the best actor Oscar) plays a modern stage actor who allows his roles to take over his personality. While playing Othello on Broadway, he starts to equate real people and situations with the characters and events of the play, and ends up killing a young woman in the same manner in which he "kills" Desdemona each night on the stage. Available on video and highly recommended.

21. Epstein, *The Friendly Shakespeare,* p. 372.

CHAPTER 1

The Plot, Setting, Language, and Imagery of *Othello*

READINGS ON
OTHELLO

The Story of *Othello*

Charles and Mary Lamb

Charles Lamb was a well-known and respected English poet, critic, and essayist who helped spark the international nineteenth-century revival of interest in Elizabethan drama through his writings about Shakespeare and the great playwright's contemporaries. In 1806, Charles and his sister, Mary, penned their now-famous *Tales from Shakespeare*, retellings of the stories of Shakespeare's best-known plays, their intention being to introduce these classics to English schoolchildren. The Lambs' elegantly written summaries soon became minor classics in their own right and have been frequently republished and widely read ever since. Following is a slightly shortened version of their retelling of Shakespeare's great play about the destructive powers of jealousy, *Othello*.

Brabantio, the rich senator of Venice, had a fair daughter, the gentle Desdemona. She was sought by divers suitors, both on account of her many virtuous qualities, and for her rich expectations. But among the suitors of her own clime and complexion, she saw none whom she could affect: for this noble lady, who regarded the mind more than the features of men, with a singularity rather to be admired than imitated, had chosen for the object of her affections, a Moor, a black, whom her father loved, and often invited to his house. . . .

He was a soldier, and a brave one; and by his conduct in bloody wars against the Turks, had risen to the rank of general in the Venetian service, and was esteemed and trusted by the state.

He had been a traveller, and Desdemona (as is the manner of ladies) loved to hear him tell the story of his adventures, which he would run through from his earliest recollection; the battles, sieges, and encounters, which he had

Reprinted from *Tales of Shakespeare*, by Charles and Mary Lamb (London, 1906).

passed through; the perils he had been exposed to by land and by water; his hair-breadth escapes, when he had entered a breach, or marched up to the mouth of a cannon; and how he had been taken prisoner by the insolent enemy, and sold to slavery . . . and how he escaped: all these accounts, added to the narration of the strange things he had seen in foreign countries. . . . These travellers' stories would so enchain the attention of Desdemona, that if she were called off at any time by household affairs, she would despatch with all haste that business, and return, and with a greedy ear devour Othello's discourse. . . .

Neither Othello's colour nor his fortune were such that it could be hoped Brabantio would accept him for a son-in-law. He had left his daughter free; but he did expect that, as the manner of noble Venetian ladies was, she would choose ere long a husband of senatorial rank or expectations; but in this he was deceived; Desdemona loved the Moor, though he was black, and devoted her heart and fortunes to his valiant parts and qualities. . . .

OTHELLO DEFENDS HIMSELF BEFORE THE SENATE

Their marriage, which, though privately carried, could not long be kept a secret, came to the ears of the old man, Brabantio, who appeared in a solemn council of the senate, as an accuser of the Moor Othello, who by spells and witchcraft (he maintained) had seduced the affections of the fair Desdemona to marry him, without the consent of her father, and against the obligations of hospitality.

At this juncture of time it happened that the state of Venice had immediate need of the services of Othello, news having arrived that the Turks with mighty preparation had fitted out a fleet, which was bending its course to the island of Cyprus, with intent to regain that strong post from the Venetians, who then held it; in this emergency the state turned its eyes upon Othello, who alone was deemed adequate to conduct the defence of Cyprus against the Turks. So that Othello, now summoned before the senate, stood in their presence at once as a candidate for a great state employment, and as a culprit, charged with offences which by the laws of Venice were made capital.

The age and senatorial character of old Brabantio, commanded a most patient hearing from that grave assembly; but the incensed father conducted his accusation with so much intemperance, producing likelihoods and allegations for proofs, that, when Othello was called upon for his defence, he had only to relate a plain tale of the course of his love; which he did with such an artless eloquence, recounting the whole story of his wooing . . . and delivered his speech with so noble a plainness (the evidence of truth), that the duke, who sat as chief judge, could not help confessing that a tale so told would have won his daughter too. . . .

This statement of Othello was confirmed by the testimony of the Lady Desdemona herself, who appeared in court, and professing a duty to her father for life and education, challenged leave of him to profess a yet higher duty to her lord and husband, even so much as her mother had shown in preferring him (Brabantio) above *her* father.

The old senator, unable to maintain his plea, called the Moor to him with many expressions of sorrow, and, as an act of necessity, bestowed upon him his daughter, whom, if he had been free to withhold her (he told him), he would with all his heart have kept from him; adding, that he was glad at soul that he had no other child. . . .

CASSIO AND IAGO

This difficulty being got over, Othello . . . readily undertook the management of the wars in Cyprus: and Desdemona, preferring the honour of her lord (though with danger) before the indulgence of those idle delights in which new-married people usually waste their time, cheerfully consented to his going.

No sooner were Othello and his lady landed in Cyprus, than news arrived that a desperate tempest had dispersed the Turkish fleet, and thus the island was secure from any immediate apprehension of an attack. But the war, which Othello was to suffer, was now beginning; and the enemies, which malice stirred up against his innocent lady, proved in their nature more deadly than strangers or infidels.

Among all the general's friends no one possessed the confidence of Othello more entirely than Cassio. Michael Cassio was a young soldier . . . amorous, and of pleasing address, favourite qualities with women; he was handsome and eloquent, and exactly such a person as might alarm the jealousy of a man advanced in years (as Othello in some measure was), who had married a young and beautiful wife; but Othello was as free from jealousy as he was noble, and as incapable of suspecting as of doing a base action. He had employed this Cassio in his love affair with Desdemona, and Cassio had been a sort of go-between in his suit: for Othello, fearing that himself had not those soft parts of conversation which please ladies, and finding these qualities in his friend, would often depute Cassio to go (as he phrased it) a-courting for him. . . . So that no wonder, if next to Othello himself . . . the gentle Desdemona loved and trusted Cassio. . . .

Othello had lately promoted Cassio to be the lieutenant, a place of trust, and nearest to the general's person. This promotion gave great offence to Iago, an older officer who thought he had a better claim than Cassio, and would often ridicule Cassio as a fellow fit only for the company of ladies, and one that knew no more of the art of war or how to set an army in array for battle, than a girl. Iago hated Cassio, and he hated Othello, as well for favouring Cassio, as for an unjust suspicion, which he had lightly taken up against Othello, that the Moor was too fond of Iago's wife, Emilia. From these imaginary provocations, the plotting mind of Iago conceived a horrid scheme of revenge, which should involve both Cassio, the Moor, and Desdemona, in one common ruin.

OTHELLO DISCIPLINES CASSIO

Iago was artful, and had studied human nature deeply, and he knew that of all the torments which afflict the mind of man (and far beyond bodily torture) the pains of jealousy were the most intolerable, and had the sorest sting. If he could succeed in making Othello jealous of Cassio, he thought it would be an exquisite plot of revenge, and might end in the death of Cassio or Othello, or both; he cared not.

The arrival of the general and his lady, in Cyprus, meeting with the news of the dispersion of the enemy's fleet, made a sort of holiday in the island. Everybody gave themselves up to feasting and making merry. Wine flowed in abundance, and cups went round to the health of the black Othello, and his lady the fair Desdemona.

Cassio had the direction of the guard that night, with a charge from Othello to keep the soldiers from excess in drinking, that no brawl might arise, to fright the inhabitants, or disgust them with the new-landed forces. That night Iago began his deep-laid plans of mischief: under colour of loyalty and love to the general, he enticed Cassio to make rather too free with the bottle (a great fault in an officer upon guard). Cassio for a time resisted, but he could not long hold out against the honest freedom which Iago knew how to put on, but kept swallowing glass after glass (as Iago still plied him with drink and encouraging songs), and Cassio's tongue ran over in praise of the Lady Desdemona, whom he again and again toasted, affirming that she was a most exquisite lady: until at last the enemy which he put into his mouth stole away his brains; and upon some provocation given him by a fellow whom Iago had set on, swords were drawn, and Montano, a worthy officer, who interfered to appease the dispute, was wounded in the scuffle. The riot now began to be general, and Iago, who had set on foot the mischief, was foremost in spreading the alarm, causing the castle-bell to be rung (as if some dangerous mutiny instead of a slight drunken quarrel had arisen). The alarm-bell ringing awakened Othello, who, dressing in a hurry, and coming to the scene of action questioned Cassio of the cause. Cassio was now come to himself, the effect of the wine having a little gone off, but was too much ashamed to reply; and Iago, pretending a great reluctance to accuse Cassio, but, as it were, forced into it by Othello, who insisted to know the truth, gave an account of the whole matter (leaving out his own share in it, which Cassio was too far gone to remember) in such a manner, as while he seemed to make Cassio's offence less, did indeed make it appear greater than it was. The result was, that Othello, who was a strict observer of discipline, was compelled to take away Cassio's place of lieutenant from him.

Thus did Iago's first artifice succeed completely; he had now undermined his hated rival, and thrust him out of his place: but a further use was hereafter to be made of the adventure of this disastrous night.

BEWARE OF JEALOUSY

Cassio, whom this misfortune had entirely sobered, now lamented to his seeming friend Iago that he should have been such a fool as to transform himself into a beast. He was undone, for how could he ask the general for his place again? he would tell him he was a drunkard. He despised himself. Iago, affecting to make light of it, said, that he, or any man living, might be drunk upon occasion; it remained now to make the best of a bad bargain; the general's wife was now the general, and could do anything with Othello; that he were best to apply to the Lady Desdemona to mediate for him with her lord; that she was of a frank, obliging disposition, and would readily undertake a good office of this sort, and set Cassio right again in the general's favour; and then this crack in their love would be made stronger than ever. A good advice of Iago, if it had not been given for wicked purposes. . . .

Cassio did as Iago advised him, and made application to the Lady Desdemona, who was easy to be won over in any honest suit; and she promised Cassio that she should be his solicitor with her lord, and rather die than give up his cause. This she immediately set about in so earnest and pretty a manner, that Othello, who was mortally offended with Cassio, could not put her off. When he pleaded delay, and that it was too soon to pardon such an offender, she would not be beat back, but insisted that it should be the next night, or the morning after, or the next morning to that at farthest. Then she showed how penitent and humbled poor Cassio was, and that his offence did not deserve so sharp a check. . . . Othello could deny nothing to such a pleader, and only requesting that Desdemona would leave the time to him, promised to receive Michael Cassio again in favour.

It happened that Othello and Iago had entered into the room where Desdemona was, just as Cassio, who had been imploring her intercession, was departing at the opposite door: and Iago, who was full of art, said in a low voice, as if to himself, "I like not that." Othello took no great notice of what he said; indeed, the conference which immediately took place with his lady put it out of his head; but he remembered it afterwards. For when Desdemona was gone, Iago, as if for mere satisfaction of his thought, questioned Othello whether Michael Cassio, when Othello was courting his lady, knew of his love. To this the general answering in the affirmative, and adding, that he had gone between them very often during the courtship, Iago knitted his brow, as if he had got fresh light on some terrible matter, and cried, "Indeed!" This brought into Othello's mind the words which Iago had let fall upon entering the room, and seeing Cassio with Desdemona; and he began to think there was some meaning in all this: for he deemed Iago to be a just man, and full of love and honesty . . . and Othello prayed Iago to speak what he knew, and to give his worst thoughts words. . . . Then Iago went on to say, what a pity it were, if any trouble should arise to Othello out of his imperfect observations; that it would not be for Othello's peace to know his thoughts; that people's good names were not to be taken away for slight suspicions; and when Othello's curiosity was raised almost to distraction with these hints and scattered words, Iago, as if in earnest care for Othello's peace of mind, besought him to beware of jealousy: with such art did this villain raise suspicions in the unguarded Othello, by the very caution which he pretended to give him against suspicion. "I know," said Othello, "that my wife is fair, loves company and feasting, is free of speech, sings, plays, and dances well: but where virtue is, these qualities are virtuous. I must have proof before I think her dishonest." Then Iago, as if glad that Othello was slow to believe ill of his lady, frankly declared that he had no proof but begged Othello to observe her behaviour well. . . . Then he artfully insinuated that Desdemona deceived her father in marrying with Othello, and carried it so closely, that the poor old man thought that witchcraft had been used. Othello was much moved with this argument, which brought the matter home to him, for if she had deceived her father, why might she not deceive her husband?

THE HANDKERCHIEF

Iago begged pardon for having moved him; but Othello, assuming an indifference, while he was really shaken with inward grief at Iago's words, begged him to go on, which Iago did with many apologies, as if unwilling to produce anything against Cassio, whom he called his friend: he then came strongly to the point, and reminded Othello how Desdemona had refused many suitable matches of her own clime and complexion, and had married him, a Moor, which showed unnatural in her, and proved her to have a headstrong will; and when her better judgment returned, how probable it was she should fall upon comparing Othello with the fine forms and clear white complexions of the young Italians her countrymen. He concluded with advising Othello to put off his reconcilement with Cassio a little longer, and in the meanwhile to note with what earnestness Desdemona should intercede in his behalf; for that much would be seen in that. So mischievously did this artful villain lay his plots to turn the gentle qualities of this innocent lady into her destruction, and make a net for her out of her own goodness to entrap her: first setting Cassio on to entreat her mediation, and then out of that very mediation contriving stratagems for her ruin.

The conference ended with Iago's begging Othello to account his wife innocent, until he had more decisive proof; and Othello promised to be patient; but from that moment the deceived Othello never tasted content of mind. . . . He no longer took delight in arms. His heart, that used to be roused at the sight of troops, and banners, and battle-array, and would stir and leap at the sound of a drum, or a trumpet, or a neighing war-horse, seemed to have lost all that pride and ambition which are a soldier's virtue; and his military ardour and all his old joys forsook him. Sometimes he thought his wife honest, and at times he thought her not so; sometimes he thought Iago just, and at times he thought him not so; then he would wish that he had never known of it; he was not the worse for her loving Cassio, so long as he knew it not: torn to pieces with these distracting thoughts, he once laid hold on Iago's throat, and demanded proof of Desdemona's guilt, or threatened instant death for his having belied her. Iago, feigning indignation that his honesty should be taken for a vice, asked Othello, if he had not sometimes seen a handkerchief spotted with strawberries in his wife's hand. Othello answered, that he had given her such a one, and that it was his first gift. "That same handkerchief," said Iago, "did I see Michael Cassio this day wipe his face with." "If it be as you say," said Othello, "I will not rest till a wide revenge swallow them up: and first, for a token of your fidelity, I expect that Cassio shall be put to death within three days; and for that fair devil (meaning his lady), I will withdraw and devise some swift means of death for her.". . .

A handkerchief of his wife's seen in Cassio's hand, was motive enough to the deluded Othello to pass sentence of death upon them both, without once inquiring how Cassio came by it. Desdemona had never given such a present to Cassio, nor would this constant lady have wronged her lord with doing so naughty a thing as giving his presents to another man; both Cassio and Desdemona were innocent of any offence against Othello: but the wicked Iago . . . had made his wife (a good, but a weak woman) steal this handkerchief from Desdemona, under pretence of getting the work [design] copied, but in reality to drop it in Cassio's way, were he might find it, and give a handle to Iago's suggestion that it was Desdemona's present.

OTHELLO ACCUSES DESDEMONA

Othello, soon after meeting his wife, pretended that he had a headache (as he might indeed with truth), and desired her to lend him her handkerchief to hold to his temples. She did so. "Not this," said Othello, "but that handkerchief I gave you." Desdemona had it not about her (for indeed it was stolen, as we have related). "How?" said Othello. . . . Desdemona . . . plainly perceived she had lost it, and with it, she feared, the affections of her husband. Then Othello started, and looked as if he were going to do some rash thing, and still he demanded the handkerchief, which when she could not produce, she tried to divert her husband from too serious thoughts, and cheerfully told him she saw all his talk about the handkerchief was only to put her off from her suit about Michael Cassio, whom she went on to praise (as Iago had foretold), till Othello in perfect distraction burst out of the room, and then Desdemona, though unwillingly, began to suspect that her lord was jealous.

What cause she could have ministered to him she knew not, and then she accused herself for accusing the noble Othello, and thought to be sure that some untoward news from Venice, or some state troubles had puddled his spirits, and made his temper not so sweet as formerly. And she said, "Men are not gods, and we must not look for that observance from them when they are married, which they show us on the bridal day.". . .

Again Othello and Desdemona met, and he accused her more plainly of being unfaithful, and of loving another man, but he did not name whom: and Othello wept, and Desdemona said, "Alas! the heavy day! why do you weep?" And Othello told her, he could have borne all sorts of evils with fortitude—poverty, and disease, and disgrace; but her infidelity had broken his heart: and he called her a weed, that looked so fair, and smelled so sweet, that the sense ached at it; and wished she had never been born. And when he had left her, this innocent lady was so stupefied with wonder at her lord's untrue suspicion of her, that a weightlike sleep came over her, and she only desired her attendant to make her bed, and to lay her wedding-sheets upon it. . . .

MURDER AND SUICIDE

Desdemona being retired to bed expecting her lord would follow her, soon fell into a slumber, the effect of her troubled spirits, when Othello entered the chamber, full of the black purpose which he had meditated of putting his lady to death. But when he saw her asleep, he thought he would not shed her blood, nor scar that white skin of hers, more white than alabaster. But he was resolved she should die; else (as he said) she would live to betray more men, as she had done him. Then he kissed her for the last time (as he said), and that kiss was so sweet, that he must needs kiss her again: and he wept, but he said they were cruel tears.

Desdemona was awakened with his kisses, and she looked upon Othello, and she saw him gnaw his underlip, and roll his eyes, and she knew he was always fatal when he looked so: and he bade her prepare for death, and to say her prayers, for he would not kill her soul. And this innocent wife, as she lay at his mercy, begged for compassion, and to know her fault, and then he named Cassio, and the handkerchief which (he said) she had given him; and as the guiltless lady was proceeding to clear herself he suddenly would hear no more, but covering her up in the bedclothes, stifled her till she died.

In this instant of time was brought into the house Cassio, wounded and bleeding, whom Iago had set one of his creatures on to assassinate; but the fellow not succeeding in his attempt to kill Cassio (whom he wounded, but not mortally), and being himself killed by Iago to prevent discovery, in his pockets were found certain letters, which made the guilt of Iago, and the innocence of Cassio, clear beyond all doubt; and Cassio now came to beg pardon of Othello, and to ask wherein he had offended him, that he had employed Iago to murder him.

This discovery was as a thunderstroke to Othello, who now plainly saw that he was no better than a murderer, and that his wife (poor innocent lady) had been ever faithful to him; the extreme anguish of which discovery making life insupportable, he fell upon his sword, and throwing himself upon the body of his dear injured lady, expired.

These rash acts raised much passion of horror and amazement in the bystanders, for Othello had borne a fair reputation, and till he was wrought upon by the arts of a villain, which his own noble nature never gave him leave to suspect, he was a loving and a doting husband. He had loved not wisely, but too well; and his manly eyes (when he learned his mistake), though not used to weep on every small occasion, dropped tears. . . . And when he was dead all his former merits and his valiant acts were remembered. Nothing now remained for his successor but to put the utmost censure of the law in force against Iago, who was executed with strict tortures; and to send word to the state of Venice of the lamentable death of their renowned general.

Local Color and Other Elements of Setting in *Othello*

John W. Draper

As explained in this essay by John W. Draper, a Shakespearean scholar who has lectured extensively in Europe, the two regions used by the playwright as primary settings for *Othello* are Venice (on the coast of northeastern Italy) and Cyprus (the large island south of what is now Turkey). The Italian city of Florence and the lands of North Africa are also alluded to in the play. Draper discusses at length Shakespeare's references to the canals, buildings, clothes, government, and dominions (territories) of fifteenth- and sixteenth-century Venice. He points out that the bard was often vague or mistaken in portraying these elements of setting, obviously due in part to the fact that Shakespeare had never been to Venice. More important in this regard, in Draper's view, is that Shakespeare was much more concerned with making his characters believable as living, breathing people than in dwelling on the details of exotic places and customs, which would have distracted his audiences from the central action of the play.

Though most Elizabethans were still Mediæval and very insular, voyages of discovery and increasing foreign trade had given City men a keener sense of foreign lands; and the Renaissance was broadening the perceptions of the intellectuals and of the aristocracy. . . . And an increasing number of merchants and nobles knew Italy at first hand. On the whole, however, the drama, even after England had a foreign king who was trying to cut a figure in international affairs, was mainly English in its local color, no matter where

Reprinted from *The "Othello" of Shakespeare's Audience*, by John W. Draper (Paris: Marcel Didier, 1952).

the scene was laid; and just a few obvious touches, usually early in the play, served to give verisimilitude [a feeling of realism] of time and place. . . . To the Elizabethans, Venice was at once a definite reality and a land of dreams; and, by the time that Shakespeare wrote *Othello*, an Elizabethan audience would doubtless expect to find in a Venetian play some reflection both of the reality and of the dream. Just how much of this reality did Shakespeare give them? Just how exactly did he depict this city that had long since fallen from its commercial supremacy, but still lived on its past glories as the pleasure-capital of Europe?

TWO MAJOR SETTINGS

The earliest interpretations of Shakespeare date from the Restoration Period [ca. 1660–1668] and the eighteenth century; and, though times had changed considerably since the spacious days of Elizabeth and James, these critics . . . recognized at least in a general way, Shakespeare's pervasive realism; but they considered it realism to human nature rather than a detailed local color, English or foreign. The nineteenth century, likewise, all too rarely applied to the plays its growing scholarship on English and Continental social life; and thus the detailed realism of Shakespeare's dramas to the times and places of the action has only recently received systematic study. *Othello* has two major settings, Venice and Cyprus . . . and by implication at least two minor settings, Florence, the background of Cassio, and North Africa and the Levant, the backgrounds of the Moor. The first act is set in Venice, and the other four in Cyprus during the brief period when Venice held that island; all the major characters but two, and presumably all the minor but the "Cyprus gallants" seem to be Venetian-born, and even Cassio and Othello are Venetians by adoption: Venice, therefore, supplies the background—ancient, romantic, gorgeous Venice, with its secretive government so different from the rest of Europe, at least half Oriental, at once an Italian state and a sea-dominion of far-flung islands, mercantile rather than feudal, and yet most aristocratic, and even late in the seventeenth century in its decadence of wealth and power, still called "Venice the Rich". On the Elizabethan stage the very name of Venice was "good theatre"; and when the play was first presented in 1604 the resumption of diplomatic relations between England and the Signiory [governing power

of the Venetian State] made this setting especially timely. . . .
The African background of Othello has been discussed in general terms, partly to settle the question of his race and color,
and partly to determine how far his jealousy, in the words of
[German translator and critic August] Schlegel, expresses "the
wild nature of that glowing zone which generates the most
raging beasts of prey and the most deadly poisons". Cyprian
and Florentine backgrounds have generally been neglected.
Indeed, it seems time to bring together with such additions as
are possible, the known material on the local color of the play,
Venetian, Cyprian, Florentine and African.

VENETIAN BUILDINGS AND CLOTHES

In Cinthio's story, the Venetian background amounts to little
more than the mere name of Venice; and, therefore, the details of setting in Shakespeare's play would seem to be
Shakespeare's own. Both books and travellers made Venice
real to the Elizabethans; and most young noblemen had had
their fling there on the Grand Tour in Italy. *The Merchant of
Venice* has the Rialto and a carnival and Jews distinguished
by a special garb—all vivid details of daily city life. *Othello*
has, to be sure, a "gondolier"; but he, and the canals on
which he earns his living, seem immediately to be forgotten
when the "several quests" that search for the Moor apparently go about the streets on foot. Desdemona is said to have
fled with this "gondolier", and yet in front of her father's
house; is solid ground for Iago and Roderigo to stand on; and
the whole play contains no mention of canals or any such
waterways. Venice, moreover, had, on the Grand Canal
alone, two hundred palaces "fit to entertain a King"; but apparently the proud Brabantio lived merely in a "house"; but
perhaps Shakespeare was dignifying the word from its use
for York House and Somerset House in London. The only
other building mentioned is the much-debated "Sagitary",
where Desdemona stays after the elopement; and more than
a century of conflicting commentary leaves one with . . .
[the] suggestion that it is the name of an inn, and probably a
pure invention of Shakespeare's. . . .

Venice was a centre not only of culture but also of fashion;
but Shakespeare ignores distinctive Venetian dress; and indeed the play has been presented with the greatest variety of
costume. In Venice, European, Oriental and perhaps African
apparel was to be seen on the streets; and the residents

themselves more or less followed sumptuary laws, that prescribed everyone's attire from the red and yellow of the professional harlot to the rich gowns, fixed by law as to cut and color, of political dignitaries, the bright uniforms of soldiers, and the simple black or elaborate vestments of the ecclesiastics [priests and religious scholars]. Nowhere does Shakespeare refer to the distinctive garb of the Doge [head government official] or the Council; Othello's "helm" might have been worn by any soldier in Europe; and the one hint of distinctive Venetian dress is Iago's reference to Brabantio's "gown", which Senators were supposed always to wear in public; but Iago's summons had wakened Brabantio in such haste that he appears without it. . . . In short, Shakespeare's only reference to the physical aspects of the city, despite the fame of its canals and buildings, is the "Sagitary"—apparently an inn that he invented for the occasion; and, despite the city's fame as a centre of fashion and despite the foreign costumes and the ceremonial robes, lay and clerical, that thronged its streets, Shakespeare's text offers merely a passing reference without descriptive detail to Brabantio's "gown". By the way, one might remark that if Shakespeare had ever been in Venice, he surely would have described that city with something of the vivid detail that he gave to London life.

VENICE'S GOVERNMENT AND DOMINIONS

Shakespeare's conception of the Venetian government . . . is almost entirely mistaken: in fact, the titular head of the state is never properly addressed as *Serenity* throughout the play; and . . . Shakespeare refers to him as a "Duke", as if he were a semi-independent feudal ruler in the Holy Roman Empire like the Duke of Milan or the Duke of Bavaria and an autocrat within his own dominion. But Venice claimed independence of the Western Empire; and the Doge had no power except his vote on various governing boards and councils. Shakespeare does mention the *Signiory;* but he seems to have had no idea of its dominant position in the state. . . . Iago's allusion to the Duke's "double" vote is also dubious; for his remark is clearly based on a misconception: the Doge had a double vote only in the general elections in which it hardly mattered, and not, as some Elizabethans seem to have thought, in any of the boards and committees that actually ruled the state. Thus Iago's statement that Brabantio had an influence in the Council equal to the Duke's two votes is based on a misunderstanding. As regards the Venetian judicial system, the tragedy is no better; for it portrays the Duke presiding like a Mediæval suzerain over the detailed administration of justice. As a matter of fact, even in the Middle Ages, the Venetians had developed an elaborate system of law courts; and Venetian justice had become famous. Plaintiff and defendant appeared at separate sittings of the court, and both had the right of appeal to higher tribunals; before the law, nobles had no advantage from their station; to discourage bribery in civil suits, the judges were forbidden to receive even visits from the contending parties or their friends; prisoners might have two counsels for their defense; and an hourglass was set on the table so that the advocates for each side would have exactly equal time for pleading. Strict ceremony ruled; and one cannot imagine a Venetian court conducted in the offhand way that the Duke settles the case of Desdemona's elopement, with all its problems of canon as well as civil law.

Shakespeare's depiction of the extent of the Venetian dominions is more accurate. Doubtless from Cinthio, he knew that the Venetians had for a while held the strategic island of Cyprus, though they had lost it to the Turks some thirty years before Shakespeare wrote the play. Othello's reference to "the Seas worth" perhaps points to the great carrying trade of Venice. Rather clearer, though sometimes disputed, is the allusion to the "Noble ship of Venice . . . *A Verenessa*". The feminine form of the word seems to show that it refers to the ship, and not, as some critics have suggested, to Cassio; and, that being the case, Shakespeare seems to have realized that Verona had become one of the dependencies of Venice on the mainland. The city . . . was an important riverport and naval station. . . . In short, the play shows little or no conception of the Venetian government and courts, but some understanding of the extent of Venetian territories.

MILITARY AND SOCIAL CUSTOMS

In that age, army and navy personnel were interchangeable; and Othello would command the ship that bore him to Cyprus, though the play does not make this clear. His appointment as a foreigner follows actual Venetian policy; for the Venetians, fearing that a victorious citizen might take advantage of his popularity to sieze supreme power . . . always put a foreigner in command, and preferably a foreigner who, like Othello, belonged to a country that was also fighting the Turks; and Shakespeare glances at this when the Duke tells Othello: "we must straight employ you Against the generall Enemy *Ottoman*". In several respects, however, the military, background is quite wrong: Othello should have been elected by the Grand Council of all the voters, and not appointed by the Duke or his Privy Council. . . . The lack of profanity in the play might be imputed to Shakespeare's knowledge of the Venetian laws against swearing even in the army—laws that could hardly be enforced—; but a more obvious explanation is the Statute of Oaths passed by Parliament about the time that Shakespeare was writing his tragedy. Indeed, the military background shows little that is characteristically Venetian.

The manners and customs reflected in the text are occasionally typical of Venice; and one might examine the two chief Venetian characters Iago and Desdemona. The former would seem to be a characteristic Italian—or at least he was what many Elizabethans considered characteristic. Desdemona, however, appears in two diverse aspects: her naïve innocence in the later acts may well reflect the strict upbringing and the exemplary morals for which wellborn Venetian girls were known; but the Desdemona of Act I is more like the independent Elizabethan woman: her free and easy entertainment of Othello in the pre-play had no place in Venice where unmarried girls were brought up "rigorously" in a "seclusion" almost Oriental; marriage, moreover, was contracted with much financial dickering and great pomp and ceremonial, and was legally forbidden with foreigners. . . . Indeed, Desdemona legally could not even talk with Othello; nor, strictly speaking, could Brabantio invite him to his house. One detail of the elopement, however, is correct: gondoliers were used in illicit love affairs, and gondolas for secret assignations; but most of the background of Desdemona in Act I runs quite counter to Venetian custom.

In the retired quiet of Venetian domestic life, the danger of boredom required some amusement; and the Venetians foregathered for stories, riddles and parlor games. These occasions were sometimes formal and stylized. . . . The company might select a leader or "queen". . . to preside over the discussion of a set topic such as solitude or love or women. This was a sort of revival of the Greek symposium [supper party] and of the Mediæval Courts of Love. Polite conversation rose to the level of a fine art; and those present said their say with wit and compliment and quotation of "authorities"... . The formal discussion of womankind between Desdemona and Iago is perhaps the best example in Shakespeare. The topic is age-old; and the Elizabethan period yields many pamphlets that in turn satirize and defend the sex. Shakespeare uses this conversation-piece to pass Desdemona's time before Othello lands in Cyprus, quite as it might have been used in an Italian court. It is planned in the question-and-answer scheme so common in the school. Dramatically, it gives a vivid expression of Iago's cynicism and uncourtly *gaucherie* [awkwardness], for it certainly is no compliment to Desdemona's sex; and Cassio ends it by excusing Iago as a bluff soldier rather than a "scholar"... .

ODDS AND ENDS OF LOCAL COLOR

Shakespeare's details of Venetian local color are a strange congeries of odds and ends. Altogether, the tragedy has some eight or ten items that can be classified as more or less accurate, and that at least some of the audience would have recognized. The character of Iago pervades the play; but most of these items are fragments of a single word or phrase, like the "gondolier" and Brabantio's "gown"; and they are far outnumbered by the crying omissions and errors, especially as regards the Venetian state. Quite properly, most of this local color comes from the mouths, or is associated with, the Venetian characters in the play, and especially Iago, whose pungent speech would savor of the earth earthy. The details themselves are drawn from many sides of life, the city streets and dress, government and the army and social customs. Most of them appear in Act I or early in Act II, when Shakespeare was building in his background. In *Hamlet* also, the touches of local color come early, but they are even fewer than in *Othello*; for Elizabethan dramatists were learning the value of authentic atmosphere only by degrees. Where Shakespeare borrowed these Venetian details is a matter of conjecture... . These gleanings of local color in the play may seem but insignificant odds and ends, and yet they add up to far more than the Florentine background ... in all of Shakespeare. He seems to have pictured most of his Continental cities in terms of the London that he and his audience knew—what else would his audience readily understand?—but Venice was so famous and so much visited that he depicted it with more distinctive and authentic detail than any of the rest.

CYPRUS AS A SETTING

During the centuries of her growing trade, Venice had extended her influence down the islands of the Dalmatian coast, and had conquered even parts of Greece. In 1489, the mother of the last crusading king of Cyprus, unable to defend the island against the Turks on the adjacent mainland, gave it to Venice, which ruled it rather oppressively for eighty-two years. At last in 1570, the Turks landed, finally took Nicosia and Famagusta by siege, and forced Venice to recognize their conquest. Shakespeare, however, follows the Cinthio narrative, printed in 1564 before the loss of Cyprus. Venetian ruins still appear on the island to attest the substantial character of the city's rule; but all four of the later acts of *Othello* yield hardly a detail of Cyprian local color: Shakespeare seems to know merely that the island had been Venetian and was not far from Rhodes, which, after the fall of Cyprus took the brunt of the Turkish attack. Othello lands at a seaport of obvious importance, that should be Famagusta . . . but Shakespeare does not even give the place a name. Early in *Othello*, the Doge enquires for "Marcus Luccicos", and is told that the man is in Florence: Marc*os* is of course a common Greek name; and Luccicos . . . is Greek at least in its ending; and some editors have suggested that this person whom the Duke wishes to consult in the Cyprian crisis, must be, as the termination -*os* would suggest, a Cypriote Greek. If so—and the inference seems probable—his name comprizes the only touch of Cyprian local color in the play. Other bits of Levantine setting occur in connection Othello's "trauells historie", the Hellespont, and, later in the play, the "Turbond-Turke" in Aleppo; but most of these details of deserts and mountains and fierce battles might refer quite as well to North Africa . . . and some of them seem to be taken, not necessarily at first hand, from [the ancient Roman naturalist] Pliny's *Natural History*. On the whole, the tragedy seems to get along with surprisingly little Oriental background, despite the fact that in *Twelfth Night* Shakespeare had already used even more remote, local color from Iran.

FLORENTINE TOUCHES

None of the scenes of the play is set in Florence; but the Arno city twice appears, as the present abode of Marcus Luccicos and as the home and background of Michael Cassio. Shakespeare in his plays presents two full-length studies of Florentines, Claudio in *Much Ado* [*About Nothing*] and Cassio in *Othello*; and doubtless with intention, he depicts both of these men as the Renaissance glass of fashion, of elegance and of propriety; and Florence vied with Rome and Venice as the cultural centre of Italy. Cassio, moreover, in his knowledge of mathematics and the new military science based on it, is very much the Florentine; for these changes were largely developed in Florence, and Machiavelli's *Art of War* (1520) was the primary treatise in the movement. Cassio, then, as a master of the "bookish" theory of war and an up-to-date officer of the new artillery, was typically Florentine. Iago's slurring references, furthermore, to Cassio as "Debitor and Creditor" and "Counter-caster" seem to refer to the fame of his native city as a banking centre; and the ruling family of the Medici had risen to their high estate largely through their financial manipulation of the public debt, so that their money and the city's and their bank's were hopelessly scrambled together. Even in Shakespeare's day, all this was not forgotten; and Henry IV of France referred to his Medici wife as "la grosse banquière" ["the great banker"]. Florence, in short, appears in the play quite correctly, as a centre of culture, of advanced military knowledge and of finance, though its sun, like that of Venice, was setting in decadence.

REFERENCES TO NORTH AFRICA

The local color of North Africa—or Barbary and Mauritania, as Iago calls it—appears but little in the play, though English merchants traded for horses and leather goods in Morocco. The text gives nothing of the white Moorish towns, their mosques, palaces and bazaars; it does mention "deserts idle" that Othello had seen, but these need not have been in Africa. Desdemona refers to the heat of Othello's native sun; and Othello's complexion is repeatedly termed "black": indeed, some critics have contended that he was a negro, and a few actors have so presented him upon the stage; and Schlegel and his followers have explained his character as that of a Noble Barbarian whose innate savagery breaks through its coating of Venetian polish. One might enquire whether the Barbary states were any more savage than was Europe in 1600. Shakespeare seems to have realized that, unlike "Negro-land" [i.e., equatorial Africa], they were organized monarchies, for Othello is descended from men of "royal siege"; and the playwright also understands that the

Berbers and the Venetians had a common enemy in the Turks who were at that time extending their dominion across North Africa—the "generall Enemy *Ottoman*". The reference to Othello's commencing soldier at seven, as if he were a page of Mediæval Europe, suggests that Shakespeare inadvertently transplanted to North Africa the decaying feudalism of the Elizabethan nobility. The reference to Othello's "baptism" raises a curious question: presumably, he had become a Christian when he entered the service of Venice; by birth, he must have been a Moslem; but here, as elsewhere, Shakespeare ignores Islam: such key words of local color as *Mohommed, Koran* and *mosque* appear nowhere in his plays; he seems vaguely to include the Moslems, along with other non-Christians, as merely *pagan*, very much as the Old French crusaders called them *paynim*; and, by implication, Brabantio refers to Othello's background as pagan. . . .

ABOVE ALL A *MAN*

Indeed, the non-Venetian local color in the play is rather slight, and some of it dubious at that: a Greek-Cyprian proper name, given partly in Latin form, three or four Levantine place-names, a glance at Florence as a city of culture, banking and the military arts; the heat of the African sun and the swarthy tan it gives, the Barbary kingdoms falling one by one before the Turks. All this is but fragmentary and superficial. Surely Turkey and Barbary merchants in London could have given him a plethora of pictorial details and endless facts about trade and government such as a modern Hollywood producer would use to the full, or over-full. Shakespeare, however, was not a geographer, or a Hollywood producer, but a dramatist; as such, his emphasis was on *men* rather than mere *things*; and, even in Venice, the most alluring of all settings to the Elizabethan, he contented himself with a minimum of mere external trappings, and either did not trouble to inform himself further, or sacrificed his representation of the government and the courts and even of the city itself, to speed the action of the play; and his most sustained effects of local color are, in the characters of Venetian soldier Iago, the Florentine gentleman Cassio and perhaps the African Othello, who, like the Moors was easily made jealous. Venice itself was full of vivid contrasts of nationalities and types; and Shakespeare could have made these contrasts the centre of his play; but he preferred to deal in very human nature, and made Othello, not merely a Moor, but above all a *man*, his Moorish qualities suggested but subordinate. Therefore, the playwright does not retard action or obscure character with more than a scattering of authentic outward detail; and, for the rest, he uses the contemporary England that his audience knew and that need not be explained. Setting, to Shakespeare, was merely setting *for a play.*

The setting of *Othello*, though it consists of mere occasional touches, is an important adjunct of the tragedy. It adds romantic glamor to make up for the Elizabethans', lack of scenery; for Venice was the city of dreams, and the Levant a land of gorgeousness and wonder. The setting also motivates both character and plot. Othello's African birth and adventurous life, though they only in part explain his actions, certainly helped to make him what he was; and his jealousy would more easily arise in the choleric environment of war-girt Cyprus than in the relaxed atmosphere of Venice. Cassio is the learned and cultivated Florentine; and the Doge and the magnificoes, though the government they run is not at all Venetian, are fitting rulers of a body politic that was famous for its shrewd efficiency. The lapses in detailed local color after all are but trifles. To its Elizabethan audience, the tragedy depicted the very essence of contemporary life in Mediterranean countries; the characters, if not quite true to fact, were at least calculated to the meridian of Elizabethan knowledge; and their actions fitted their vivid personalities so that they seemed drawn to the very life.

Shakespeare's Use of Language Defines the Play's Main Characters

Norman Sanders

The characters of Othello and his ensign, Iago (as well as Desdemona and other characters), are in large part defined by the kinds of words and speeches they employ and the images their respective language conveys to the reader/spectator. As University of Tennessee scholar and noted Shakespearean editor Norman Sanders points out, Shakespeare endows each character with his own verbal idioms (word forms or expressions peculiar to a given language or region where it is spoken). For example, Iago's speech displays a lack of imagination and often lowbrow, repulsive vocabulary, says Sanders. By contrast, Othello's natural speech is poetic, stately, romantic, heroic, and so on; so Shakespeare achieves great effect when, during the course of the action, Iago manages to "infect" Othello with some sordid thoughts and speech, in effect bringing the noble Moor partway down to his own level. Sanders concludes that the play's language cannot be fully appreciated simply by reading the play, but must be experienced as part of the overall visual and auditory imagery of a stage or film production.

The blueprint Shakespeare passed to his fellows was invariably a highly-wrought verbal construct, and it is from this that our experience of the work—like theirs—must begin. This is especially true of *Othello*, in which Shakespeare seems to have used so many of the resources of the language as vehicles for deliberately designed dramatic effects.

Most immediately striking are the carefully-fashioned and quite distinct idioms he invented for his two main characters. At the most obvious level we notice that Iago uses more prose than Othello . . . one example of which is this:

> 'Tis in ourselves that we are thus or thus. Our bodies are our gardens, to the which our wills are gardeners. So that if we will plant nettles, or sow lettuce, set hyssop and weed up thyme, supply it with one gender of herbs or distract it with many, either to have it sterile with idleness or manured with industry, why the power and corrigible authority of this lies in our wills.   (1.3.313–19)

Such a style is intellectually generated; it is ingenious [clever] speech—the result of a conscious calculation of effect rather than an instinctive utterance springing unbidden from the subconscious [i.e., a natural, spontaneous expression]. . . . The symmetrically balanced sentences and phrases are an exact measure of the cool self-awareness that typifies all Iago says and does. It is . . . the style of Janus, the two-faced god by whom he swears (1.2.33).

Exactly the same qualities are to be found in his venture into improvised verse to entertain Desdemona after she has landed in Cyprus:

> She that was ever fair, and never proud,
> Had tongue at will, and yet was never loud;
> Never lacked gold, and yet went never gay;
> Fled from her wish, and yet said 'Now I may' . . .
>   (2.1.145–48)

Here, of course, Iago is deliberately acting the role of male cynic expected of him; but the poetic vehicle for his performance is ironically a true reflection of the habit of thought natural to him. . . .

A similar self-consciousness is observable in Iago's blank verse [unrhymed] speeches. Whenever he resorts to metaphor there is always a strict control of the image, a closed quality, whereby a static mental picture is evoked rather than any dynamic imaginative propulsion into some wider topic; for example:

>   but indeed my invention
> Comes from my pate as birdlime does from frieze . . .
>   (2.1.124–25)

>   the thought whereof
> Doth like a poisonous mineral gnaw my inwards . . .
>   (2.1.277–78)

Perhaps the best illustration of such imagistic narrowness occurs at the moment he reaches the peak of his control over Othello, and is moved in his triumph to attempt an imitation of the Moor's own soaring, cosmic allusiveness. But all he manages to produce is this:

> Witness you ever-burning lights above,
> You elements that clip us round about,
> Witness that here Iago doth give up
> The execution of his wit, hands, heart,
> To wronged Othello's service. . . .   (3.3.464–68)

USING SPEECH TO DEBASE AND DEGRADE

This capacity in Iago to reduce imaginatively all he contemplates is most vividly seen in those lines which convey his view of humanity. All spiritual values are debased. Love is merely an anatomical function—'carnal stings . . . a lust of the blood and a permission of the will' (1.3.322–36); reputation is 'an idle and most false imposition, oft got without merit and lost without deserving' (2.3.247–48); Cassio's modern military skills which earned him quick promotion are reduced to the activities of a grubbing book-keeper (1.1.31); Othello's romantic vision of his profession is really only a love of 'pride and purposes' manifesting itself in 'bombast circumstance, / Horribly stuffed with epithets of war' (1.1.12–14); loyalty and service are 'obsequious bondage' like that of an ass (1.2.45–8); women are things (3.3.304), guinea-hens (1.3.309), and wild-cats (2.1.109).

These last two comparisons are examples of perhaps the most repulsive aspect of Iago's vocabulary: namely his tendency to depict the world as a 'stable or malodorous menagerie'. His speech habitually degrades human activities to the level of the doings of despicable animals: he himself is a spider who will 'ensnare as great a fly as Cassio' (2.1.164) and Roderigo becomes his hunting dog to be loosed on the lieutenant (2.1.284–85); married men are but yoked beasts of burden (4.1.64–5); Othello is a Barbary horse (1.1.111–12) and an old black ram tupping the white ewe Desdemona (1.1.89–90); and the act of love is a making of a 'beast with two backs' (1.1.116).

It is, however, quite another kind of reference that moves Iago's speech. . . . All of his real life is inward. Driven by . . . self-interest, he values only those who 'Keep yet their hearts attending on themselves' (1.1.51) and considers 'soul' to be the possession only of men who 'do themselves homage' (1.1.54). As he tells us himself, he is not what he is (1.1.66): not the 'honest' blunt-spoken soldier that most characters in the play attest to his being, but rather a devil creating his own hell on earth and effecting the damnation of others. Darkness is his natural element and he dominates the three night scenes (1.1, 2.3, 5.1). He calls easily on the powers of blackness, on the 'Divinity of hell' (2.3.317); his success in trapping Cassio is recognised, as the warning bell proves his skill, with 'Diabolo, ho!' (2.3.142); 'Hell and night' form the climate that will bring his 'monstrous birth to the world's light' (1.3.385–86). He really believes that he can turn Desdemona's virtue into pitch (2.3.327), make human love into the prey of 'the green-eyed monster' of jealousy (3.3.168), and Cassio's quality of daily beauty into crass irresponsibility.

He can, of course, do none of these things; but he has the ability to do something much worse: he can make them seem to be true. This Ensign who does not show the flag of his real nature (1.1.155–56) is the master stage director who can manage his cast of players so that two nocturnal broils [night brawls] are enacted without the participants realising they are not acting spontaneously; he can verbally create a scene of adultery which can set Othello on the rack (4.1.1–34); he can put on 'heavenly shows' which are actually devilish entertainments (2.3.318–20). Even his props are not what they seem to be: the handkerchief, so emotionally loaded by Othello, is simultaneously the precious gift to Desdemona and yet a trifle light as air (3.3.323), which Cassio's possession transforms into what it is not. That which Othello does not even see clearly in Cassio's hand—'Was that mine?' (4.1.166)—becomes the ocular [visible] proof of adultery. 'Honesty' itself is in him a guise of dishonesty; and a particular kind of honesty (i.e. chastity) in Desdemona appears to be begrimed and black as Othello's face (3.3.387–89).

OTHELLO'S SPEECH INFECTED BY IAGO'S

One of the means which Shakespeare employs to indicate the gradual hold Iago develops over Othello's mind is the growing infection of his speech by Iago's vocabulary. . . . Whereas the former delights in the dualities of saint and devil, beauty and dishonesty, alabaster skin and the possibility of concealed rottenness, the latter finds such insecurity unbearable. For him 'to be once in doubt / Is once to be resolved' (3.3.181–82)—that is, to be certain of the opposite of the quality so doubted. This transference of manner of thought from man to man is commenced in an exchange in

which the words heard are only the tips of the psychological
action taking place in the sub-text:

IAGO.   My noble lord —

OTHELLO. What dost thou say, Iago?

IAGO.   Did Michael Cassio,
When you wooed my lady, know of your love?

OTHELLO. He did from first to last. Why dost thou ask?

IAGO. But for a satisfaction of my thought;
No further harm.

OTHELLO.   Why of thy thought, Iago?

IAGO. I did not think he had been acquainted with her.

OTHELLO. O yes, and went between us very oft.

IAGO. Indeed?

OTHELLO. Indeed? Ay, indeed. Discern'st thou aught in that?
Is he not honest?

IAGO. Honest, my lord?

OTHELLO. Honest? Ay, honest.

IAGO. My lord, for aught I know.

OTHELLO.   What dost thou think?

IAGO. Think, my lord?   (3.3.92–106)

Iago's habitual conception of man as animal produces in
Othello's mind a hideous vision of a bestial world inhabited
by goats, monkeys, toads, crocodiles, blood-sucking flies and
poisonous snakes. . . .

Ironically the Moor takes over too the Venetian's diabolic
vision. The mental hell he creates for himself with Iago's assistance has at its centre the 'devil' Desdemona. The prayer
for perdition to catch his soul (3.3.90–1) in his last moment
of perfect erotic security is answered by his ensign. Desdemona becomes in his eyes a 'fair devil' (3.3.479) with a de-
monically sweating palm (3.4.38), who must be 'double
damned' (4.2.36) because she is 'false as hell' (4.2.38), and
whose fate must be determined by 'black vengeance' called
from its 'hollow cell' (3.3.448) for the purpose. Her bedroom
is the inferno itself at the door of which stands her maid
Emilia as portress (4.2.89–91) and in which she must be
killed lest, Satan-like, 'she'll betray more men'(5.2.6). When
we thus consider the dimensions of the horrible conceit

wrought by Iago's suggestions in Othello's imagination there can be no greater irony in the play than what he says just prior to his total collapse: 'It is not words that shakes me thus' (4.1.40).

OTHELLO'S "MUSICAL" SPEECHES

Othello's idiomatic norm which Iago so perverts is far different from this animalistic, monstrous, diabolic universe. It is in fact one of the glories of English dramatic poetry. So much has been written about it that it is sufficient here to instance some of the characteristics of the '*Othello* music'.

The first point to be made about it is that this stately, formal, slow-moving poetry, so heavily loaded with vividly realised physicality, is the perfect vehicle for conveying to the audience the cast of mind, character and powerful emotion of this hero who is 'in life', as he tells us, rude in his speech and 'little blessed with the soft phrase of peace' (1.3.81–2). He is no more a 'poet' than any other verse-speaking character in the play; it is merely that this eloquent verbal music best exhibits the nature of the man his experience has made him. . . . There is an inward aloofness, a separation of image from image and word from word, seen clearly in a passage such as this:

O heavy hour!
Methinks it should be now a huge eclipse
Of sun and moon, and that th'affrighted globe
Should yawn at alteration.   (5.2.99–102)

Here, as elsewhere, the machinery of the universe is vividly juxtaposed with [placed beside] human experience. In a similar manner geographical spread and adventurous travel are compared, at length but distantly, with moments of powerful emotion and states of being: in the great aria describing his wooing (1.3.127–69) and in the assertion of his unswerving will (3.3.454–63). Even as he comes to face the truth in his haunting final lines, there is the same non-fusion of images, as the medicinal gum of the Arabian trees is set against the non-curative tears Othello sheds; as another ignorant pagan unknowingly throws away great wealth; and as one kind of state traitor, 'a malignant and a turbaned Turk', simply parallels the Moor himself, a far worse traducer [malicious liar] who struck down the loveliest of all Venetians (5.2.334–52).

In the theatre, the voices of [Paul] Robeson or [Godfrey]

Tearle in our own day have projected movingly the most remarkable quality of Othello's speech: its romantic, heroic,
picturesque, adventurous, exotic nature. For him life is
highly coloured. . . . War is not, as it is for Iago, a trade, but
a glorious world of tented fields, plumed troops, neighing
steeds, shrill trumps, spirit-stirring drums, and cannons
which rather 'th'immortal Jove's dread clamours counter-
feit' (3.3.349–58) than kill messily. Every facet of his life that
is susceptible to an enhancing inflation is emphasised, even
as those which cannot are relegated to being of minimum
influence and small memory. . . .

When Othello, late in life, finds in Desdemona the erotic
equivalent of his military profession, he transfers on to her
all the imaginative appreciation which had formerly been
lavished on his career. She becomes his 'fair warrior'
(2.1.174), his 'captain's captain' (2.1.74) and his camp companion. But more significant, and fatal, than this verbal mil-
itarising of his wife is his insistence on making her the sole
object of his full powers of romantic projection. She is not
only his love but Love itself which banished chaos from the
universe at the beginning of the world (3.3.90–2). Meeting
her after a frightening absence is quite literally for him the
equivalent of heaven:

> If it were now to die,
> 'Twere now to be most happy; for I fear
> My soul hath her content so absolute
> That not another comfort like to this
> Succeeds in unknown fate.   (2.1.181–85)

Just how totally unsuitable a character for the burden of
such idealisation Desdemona actually is finds expression in
her horrified response to this:

> The heavens forbid
> But that our loves and comforts should increase,
> Even as our days do grow.   (2.1.185–87)

THEATRICAL EFFECTS REINFORCE THE LANGUAGE

However, the poetry in the play is not merely a device for in-
dividualisation of character. The large language patterns in-
terweave themselves across character, mental state and particular situation. Deceitful appearance is not linked
exclusively with 'honest Iago'. Honest (i.e. chaste and truthful) Desdemona did deceive her father in wooing and marrying Othello, she does attempt to conceal from her husband

the loss of the handkerchief, and she even dies with a charitable lie upon her lips about the manner of her death. Emilia's assumption of the façade of moral cynicism (4.3.60–99) is as false as her husband's exterior and conceals a love that makes her prepared to die in the defence of truth and goodness. Othello's black countenance is to Desdemona the unattractive casing of a beautiful mind, whereas, to Roderigo, Brabantio and Iago it is the proper colouring for the devil Iago ensures he becomes. And Iago's own whiteness, quite different from the alabaster skin of Desdemona, hides a soul as black as any in the literature of the world.

This dichotomy between being and seeming is reflected in the language of blackness and whiteness, dark and light, hell and heaven that touches so many aspects of the play . . . the night hours in which Iago creates his discord and violence; and the hell of doubt and jealousy that is set against the lovers' celestial vision of their world.

Growing out of the geographical position of Venice as Europe's gateway to the exotic eastern lands is the thread of magic and witchcraft that surfaces at various points in the play. For Iago, of course, these things mean diabolic conjuring and devilish spirits to twist and pervert others. For Othello the magic in the web of the handkerchief is a symbol of the binding power of marital love (3.4.51–72), of the extent to which the gentle Desdemona has transformed his whole existence. It was by means of the witchcraft of his words that he was able to win her love, a form of enchantment her father took to be of a malignant nature (1.3.60–4, 99–106).

Naturally, none of the language in the play works in isolation, and many of its effects in their rich interrelationships can only be seen to the full when in production. Lighting, costume, sound-effects, blocking, actors' appearance, gesture and movement are all available to reinforce and develop the implications found in the verbal texture. No reading of the play, for example, can hold in the mind the blackness of Othello at *every* entrance, which a stage production conveys effortlessly with the simple application of make-up. The . . . vocabulary and imagery of trial and legal process become visually and positionally realised when we view the Senate scene (1.3) with the Duke as judge, the senators as jury, Brabantio as accuser, Othello as defendant and Desdemona as expert witness. . . .

The authority and resonance of 'Keep up your bright swords, for the dew will rust them' (1.2.59) are given an ex-

tra dimension when spoken by a white-gowned Paul Robeson with the swords pointed at his breast and the torchlight
glistening on his black skin. The sheer alienation of Othello
from his society will be held forever in the mind of the audiences who saw Laurence Olivier's cat-like, sensuous, Caribbean walk. The awful vulgarity of Iago's mind (a rarely noticed trait) was made actual when Leo McKern sat gleefully
and gloatingly across the chest of the insensible Anthony
Quayle; even as Iago's underlying twisted psyche was trans-
mitted silently in the tiny betraying gestures of Jose Ferrer as
he taunted the blundering Robeson. . . .

Of course, no single production can hope to do more than
realise some aspects of the drama's totality; even as no critical reading can attempt to do more than offer a simplified
version of the original. Both the literary and the theatrical
approaches are thus necessary and interrelated; for just as
no production can convey the intellectual grasp of the poetic
machinery of *Othello* that one can derive from . . . the
'*Othello* music', so no essay can burn into the mental ear for
a lifetime Godfrey Tearle's delivery of 'My wife, my wife!
What wife? I have no wife' (5.2.98) with its huge freight of
the despairing futility of all human aspiration.

Musical Images and References Unite the Play's Scenes and Ideas

Ros King

In this insightful essay, Ros King, a lecturer in language and literature at London's Queen Mary College, examines the plot and structure of *Othello* scene by scene. She maintains that songs, tunes, trumpets and other instruments, references to harmony and things being "in tune" or "out of tune," and other musical terms and images serve as structural elements that help to knit the plot together. For example, Iago uses songs to further his nefarious scheme, as in the scene when he gets Cassio drunk. Also, blasts of the trumpet are frequently used to signify ceremonies of state and official duties or to symbolize fame and the military, both of which figure prominently in Othello's profession and position.

> O, you are well-tuned now,
> But I'll set down the pegs that make this music,
> As honest as I am.
>
> (2.1.177–79)

Iago's commentary on the reunion of Othello and Desdemona on the island of Cyprus is more than just a fanciful statement of his intentions. Iago as a character deliberately sets out to destroy the harmony of love, but Shakespeare, the dramatist, presents his words and actions as part of an extensive pattern of musical images and effects. This pattern works integrally as a structural theme. It unites and expands the ideas of the play and provides the essential terms of reference for both aesthetic and moral judgement.

Othello probably makes more use of music than any other Shakespeare tragedy. Iago's two songs and Cassio's wind

Excerpted from Ros King, "'Then Murder's Out of Tune': The Music and Structure of *Othello*," in *Shakespeare Survey*, no. 39. Copyright © Cambridge University Press 1987. Reprinted by permission of Cambridge University Press. (Footnotes in the original have been omitted in this reprint.)

music are essential to the plot, while the 'willow song' expresses Desdemona's situation and her state of mind with accurate and agonizing economy.

Previous studies have demonstrated that Shakespeare knew and was using well-established musical theory. They show that the play contains passages which spring from such commonplaces as the superiority of string over wind instruments, the existence of 'music that cannot be heard' (the music of the spheres), and the continuing debate as to whether the performance of music was a suitable occupation for anyone who claimed to be a gentleman.

Renaissance ideas of musical harmony were inextricably bound up with order and structure. Following the ideas of [the ancient Greek thinkers] Pythagoras and Plato, Renaissance scholars believed that the simple mathematical proportions 1:2, 2:3, 3:4, which result in the intervals of perfect harmony in ancient music—the octave, the perfect fifth, and the perfect fourth—were also responsible for the beauties and numerical structure of the universe, from the 'dancing' of the tuneful planets to the form and constitution of man. Discounting folk-song and ballads, audible music on earth was considered as falling into two categories—public, outdoor ceremonial music played on 'loud' instruments by professional musicians and bandsmen (military trumpeters, drummers, and the like) and private, indoor music played on 'soft' stringed instruments (virginals, lutes, viols, etc.), sometimes by professional musicians but often by members of the upper classes for the amusement of themselves and their friends. The music in *Othello* exists in all these forms: actual and metaphorical, public and private, folk-song and art-song. It is an essential part of the way Shakespeare illustrates both the initial harmony of Othello's and Desdemona's love and the manner in which they combine their official public roles with their private lives.

OTHELLO AND DESDEMONA SHARE ROLES

As a military commander and general, Othello's life is punctuated by musical sounds—mostly played on trumpets and drums—designed to regulate life in the garrison and give orders on the battlefield. During the course of the play, the trumpets announce the arrival of first Othello and later the Venetian senator, Lodovico, before summoning all the characters to a state dinner. The trumpet is a reminder of state, ceremonial, and duty. A public instrument, it was used for broadcasting information to large numbers of people and in contemporary art . . . it had understandably become the identifying symbol for personifications of Fame.

The first reference to trumpets in the play, however, comes from Desdemona. She uses it with the connotations of both 'fame' and the 'military life' to express her love for her husband and to convince the Venetian Senate that it is fitting that she should accompany him to Cyprus:

> That I did love the Moor to live with him,
> My downright violence and storm of fortunes
> May trumpet to the world.
>
> (1.3.248–50)

The daughter 'never bold' that her father has described, demonstrates instead that she is the true partner of a man of action. She is no simple retiring maiden but a woman who is well aware of the consequences of her actions. She knows that Othello is a public figure and that by marrying him, particularly in such a 'violent' manner, she is likely to attract public attention to herself. She is not prepared to stay at home, a 'moth of peace', but is anxious to share her husband's life and to take an active role in it. Indeed, both lovers see their relationship as a reciprocal one, a partnership of mutual help and interest, and in these early scenes their descriptions of each other find similar and complementary expression:

> She loved me for the dangers I had passed,
> And I loved her that she did pity them.
>
> (1.3.167–68)

Just as Desdemona demands to share her husband's life, so Othello—perhaps even more remarkably—is willing for her to do so. Throughout the first half of the play in every speech of more than half-a-dozen lines, he manages to combine with perfect ease the most earnest consideration of state affairs with equally earnest and loving reference to his wife. . . . It is the similarity of thought and outlook, the bounty, the generosity, and the courage which each finds in the other that is important. This sharing of roles is further indicated when they meet after the storm on the island of Cyprus. He greets her as the soldier-hero and she him as the supporting lover: 'My fair warrior . . . My dear Othello' (2.1.180). The rarity of their thinking is emphasized by observations made by other characters on the same theme which are markedly rooted in sexual stereotypes. Cassio's description of Desdemona as 'Our great Captain's Captain' (2.1.74) is a recognition of Desdemona's powers in the terms of perfect woman-on-a-pedestal which in no way detracts from Othello's purely masculine authority, whereas Iago's very similar line, 'Our General's wife is now the General' (2.3.305), has exactly the opposite effect—and deliberately so. Instead of a unity in partnership, Iago depicts for his audience just another hen-pecked husband, harassed by an appalling wife.

Iago an 'Everyman'

From his observations about women to his thoughts on reputation, Iago consistently follows and exploits conventional beliefs about the way the world works. He thinks as Everyman thinks and Everyman is therefore bound to hold him in respect. . . . It is this that makes him so powerful. Audiences do not stop to disapprove of his scheming—they are too excited by it—and every character in the play (not just Othello and Desdemona) is taken in by it because in the context of normal social behaviour everything he says appears reasonable and credible even when it is most lying and pernicious.

> And what's he, then, that says I play the villain?
> When this advice is free I give and honest,
> Probal to thinking.

(2.3.325–27)

In supporting Desdemona's request to accompany him to Cyprus, Othello quite clearly is not thinking like Everyman, and it is Iago's constant task throughout the long scenes of 3.3 and 3.4 to manipulate him into thinking that way. . . .

It is evident from Iago's relationship with his own wife and from his views expressed in the rhyming game he plays with her and Desdemona that his ideas on what might be possible within marriage are very different from Othello's. In his own marriage, petty wrangling and jealousy are the norm and he is thus understandably determined to destroy the harmony and accord that his black commanding officer has found. His manner of doing this is evidenced by his behaviour in the landing-in-Cyprus scene. . . . The stage picture of an overly courteous Cassio taking Desdemona 'by the palm' and kissing his fingers (in a manner still practised by Italians wishing to impress and still regarded with suspicion and derision by Englishmen) is instantly replaced by that of Othello and Desdemona in each other's arms. Iago is the commentator on both. He perverts the former innocent though overdone courtesies to a gross anal sexuality:

> Yet again your fingers to your lips? Would they were clyster-pipes for your sake.

(2.1.175)

However, when he likens the embrace between Othello and Desdemona to a well-tuned string instrument in the passage with which this article began, he is describing no more than the truth. He demonstrates that he is capable of appreciating the extent and quality of Othello's and Desdemona's love—an essential prerequisite to attempting to destroy it.

CASSIO'S COURTESY GIVES IAGO HIS CHANCE

God's hand tuning the string of the universe is a fairly common Renaissance and Shakespearian emblem. . . . Iago does not mention a specific instrument, but the lute, a solo instrument with courses of strings tuned in consonant pairs so that two strings are plucked together and sound as one, lends itself admirably to an image of union in marriage. Such an instrument also forms the central image in Sonnet 8—one of the initial sequence urging love, marriage, and procreation—because the sound produced when both identically pitched strings are plucked together is far fuller and more resonant than either would produce singly:

> Mark how one string, sweet husband to another,
> Strikes each in each by mutual ordering;
> Resembling sire and child and happy mother,
> Who, all in one, one pleasing note do sing. . . .

One of the ways in which Iago cultivates his appearance of honesty is by pretending to the practice of harmony, and it is through music that he effects the vital first stage of his plot, the undoing of Cassio. Despite Iago's disparaging remarks, Othello has undoubtedly made the right decision in appointing Cassio to the lieutenantship. As an 'arithmetician' (1.1.19) he should know something about recent revolutionary developments in the art of fortification. The defence of Mediterranean islands at this time centred on their fortified ports, thus, rather than requiring a soldier who can 'set a squadron in the field' (1.1.22), Othello needs someone to design and build the new star-shaped defences and to calculate the track of tunnels for the laying of mines. Cassio is not, however, completely 'bookish', for during the course of the play he proves himself to be an accomplished swordsman. Both Othello and the Venetian Senate have the greatest confidence in him, and at the end of the play the governorship of the island falls to him quite naturally. Unfortunately, he has two weaknesses—a bad head for drink and a basic insecurity regarding his position in society. He presents himself as a gentleman from Florence but is slightly uneasy in the role. In his description of Desdemona to Montano (2.1.61–87), and in his manner of greeting her when she lands in Cyprus, he is seen striving just a little too hard to be courtly, and it is this excess which gives Iago his chance: 'Ay, smile upon her, do. I will gyve thee in thine own courtship' (2.1.170). This social unease is further emphasized by his ambivalent attitude to Iago's songs on the Court of Guard. He is beguiled by the music but he is also wary of it. He is not sufficiently sure of himself and his own social standing to risk behaving in what some might consider to be an improper manner. . . . By persuading Cassio to accept a drink, staging a rowdy drinking song and organizing a fight, Iago has corrupted the entire 'Court and Guard of safety'. A single drunken man might be overlooked but not a noisy brawl involving all members of the watch. Othello has decreed that the island should be free to celebrate both the sinking of the Turkish fleet and his own marriage—again a perfectly balanced combination of the public and private life—but the islanders can only do this in safety if those on watch are keeping to their duty. The decree is made in the form of a direct address by Othello's herald to the audience . . . thus bringing that audience into some measure of active involvement in the situation.

A Song to Make Cassio Forget His Duties

The original audience cannot have been ignorant of the spectacular advances of the Turks in the Mediterranean, as they were a matter for public concern and well documented. Cyprus had in fact fallen to the Turks in 1571 and Hakluyt's *Voyages* includes an eye-witness account written by a Venetian nobleman. He tells how the Venetian garrison of Famagusta eventually surrendered after a siege lasting nearly six months on promise of a safe conduct to Candy (Crete), but that the promise was not kept. Almost the entire garrison was murdered or taken as slaves and one of its commanding officers skinned alive.

Appended to *The Mahumetane or Turkish History* published in 1600 are two short tracts, 'The Narration of the Wars of Cyprus' and 'The Causes of the Greatness of the

Turkish Empire'. This last attempts an analysis of the reasons for Turkish success and concludes that, in contrast with the Turkish forces, the Christians at all levels of command were badly disciplined and too preoccupied with their own differences and jealousies:

> we are desperately diseased, even to the death, our soldiers being mutinous, factious, disobedient, who fashioned by no rules of discipline, contained in duty by no regard of punishment . . . which is as common to the captains and commanders as the private soldiers, a number of whom studying their particular revenge, their private ambition or (than which with men of war there is naught more odious) their servile gain, betray their country, neglect their princes' command and without executing aught worthy their trust and employment cause often impediments through malicious envy of another's glory, to whatsoever might be worthily executed.

In this context, it becomes clear that Shakespeare's play is very much more than the most famous story of sexual jealousy ever written. Othello's and Desdemona's love is presented as quite inseparable from their management of state affairs, while Iago's jealousy of both Cassio and Othello, and the factious quarrel which he engineers on the Court of Guard, is part of an examination of the ways in which personal rivalries can affect and be affected by wider political issues. This marks a departure from Cinthio's story [the source of the play], in which the geographical change of scene from Venice to Cyprus is incidental and bears no stated military or political significance, and where no mention is made of the Moor's ability in his public life. Shakespeare presents a man who has been entrusted with a large measure of the safety and commercial interest of the Venetian state [i.e., keeping Cyprus safe from the Turks], and who, for the first half of the play, seems capable of fulfilling that trust. Iago's plan demands a reversal of Othello's values of love and loyalty, and the first stage of this plan is effected by the drinking song directed against Cassio.

The song instructs the drinkers to forget their public duty to the wider issues and longer time-scheme of the state and to concentrate instead on the personal pleasure that one man can snatch during a single lifetime:

> A soldier's a man;
> O, man's life's but a span;
> Why, then, let a soldier drink.

> (2.3.66–68)

Cassio makes one last attempt to refer back to the public situation by proposing 'the health of our General', which Montano is quick to second; but Iago prevents the drinking of the toast by launching into a second song, 'King Stephen'.

This song is a single stanza from the middle of a traditional ballad entitled 'Bell, my wife' or 'The old cloak'. . . . The song takes the form of a conversation between the shepherd and Bell, his wife. She wants him to get up and tend the cow, taking his old cloak about him; he wants to improve his attire—and his social standing—and go to court. Eventually, to save an argument, he gives in. . . .

Iago has turned Bell's words into a praise of anarchy and dubious virtue, while as always retaining his appearance of honesty. Thus Iago uses apparent harmony in order to start the process of setting down the pegs that make the music between Desdemona and Othello. By this time almost half the play has passed, and as yet Iago has not even started to work on Othello himself.

CASSIO'S COARSE SONG

Having been undone in music, Cassio ironically reinforces his fall from favour in an attempt to create harmony. He takes it upon himself to provide the traditional musical awakening for the bride and groom on the morning after the wedding night and has hired musicians to perform this aubade. These musicians are playing wind instruments or 'pipes'. This is a neat visual and aural pun on the 'clyster pipes' that Iago has already said should be at Cassio's lips, and the bawdy jokes made by the Clown on the nature of anal wind music in this scene indicate that the connection is deliberate:

> CLOWN. O, thereby hangs a tail.
>
> MUSICIAN. Whereby hangs a tale, sir?
>
> CLOWN. Marry, sir, by many a wind instrument that I know.
>
> (3.1.8–11)

Whatever the exact identity of these musical pipes—and this of course would depend on the particular resources of the company—the instruments must have double reeds (like modern oboe reeds) which produce a nasal sound: 'Why, masters, ha' your instruments been in Naples, that they speak i' th' nose thus?' (3.1.3). Instruments of this kind might be blown directly, or attached to a bag (i.e. a bagpipe). The latter might be implied by the Clown's line 'put up your pipes in your bag' (3.1.19), while the phallic imagery could be emphasized visually by means of the distinctive upturned shape of the crumhorn.

Cassio behaves correctly in considering that music is necessary for the occasion, but he displays an inordinate lack of taste in his choice of such music. The Clown's comments indicate that it is coarse and crude and not suitable as an aubade for the newly married pair, and reports that the General would only be happy if the musicians could play music that cannot be heard. Of course neither the Clown nor the musicians take this to mean any more than that they should pack up and go away, but the line refers back to Othello and his wishes. He enjoys music. Even at the height of his rage he can be moved by the recollection that his wife 'sings, plays and dances well' (3.3.189). In desiring music that cannot be heard he is demanding the music of the spheres which is inaudible to the ears of fallen man but which alone would be a suitable accompaniment to his love for his wife.

CASTING OFF DESDEMONA

As the audible music in the play gets noticeably falser, so both Othello and Desdemona find it progressively more difficult to effect the harmony of true partnership. As her husband becomes unaccountably difficult and distant, she admits to Cassio that her 'advocation is not now in tune' (3.4.124). Similarly, as Iago drives in the wedge that alienates him from his wife, Othello finds that without her the very sounds intrinsic to his life no longer have any meaning for him:

> O, now for ever
> Farewell the tranquil mind, farewell content,
> Farewell the plumed troops and the big wars
> That makes ambition virtue. O, farewell.
> Farewell the neighing steed and the shrill trump,
> The spirit-stirring drum, th' ear-piercing fife,
> The royal banner, and all quality,
> Pride, pomp, and circumstance, of glorious war.
> And O ye mortal engines whose rude throats
> Th' immortal Jove's dread clamours counterfeit,
> Farewell. Othello's occupation's gone.
> (3.3.351–61)

The farewell to the type of music which, according to classical theory, had been thought capable of raising men to noble acts, the 'spirit-stirring drum, th' ear-piercing fife' emphasizes Othello's rejection of his public duty and demonstrates that just as with Cassio on the Court of Guard, the attack on the private man is resulting in the destruction of the public one. The terror of his situation lies in the fact that he and Desdemona had been so close that they had become indeed the 'beast with two backs', the hermaphrodite image of perfect love of which Aristophanes speaks in Plato's *Symposium* (189ff) and which Iago parodies in sexual terms in the first scene of the play (1.1.118). Thus casting off Desdemona is like trying to cut himself in half—it inevitably leads to his own destruction. Everything that he had ever lived for, including his public life established before he met Desdemona, is gone. He feels that he no longer exists, and refers to himself in the third person as 'Othello'. The long 'temptation' scene in which this speech occurs is preceded by a deceptively short and seemingly insignificant scene (3.2) in which Othello enters with his aides, dispatches a letter to the Senate, and then departs to inspect the fortifications. This is his last act of official business in the play, and it now becomes apparent that this six-line scene has marked the climax of Othello's career and that its position as the central scene of the play is a fitting one.

The fact that we, the audience, have already witnessed Iago's skilful manipulation of Cassio and Roderigo enables us to accept that his successful transformation of Othello is possible. The internal construction of act 3, scene 3 as a whole dramatizes the difficulty of Iago's task and shows the tightrope of expediency and luck on which he is walking. This scene is the longest in the play. . . . Throughout the scene, Othello keeps reiterating his belief in his wife's fidelity, a belief which is always first welcomed and then deftly punctured by Iago. By the end of the scene, the man who had been seen combining his domestic and public life with ease—receiving and giving orders with Desdemona by his side, controlling his men and inspecting defences with a quiet because absolute authority—can now think of nothing except his wife's body and her supposed faithlessness, which eventually he comes to 'see' as clearly as if he had indeed the 'ocular proof' which he demands from Iago. . . . Iago's disparagement and suspicion of Desdemona's musical and other qualities is almost immediately challenged by the sound of a Venetian trumpet. Desdemona enters, fulfilling both her official duties and her family ones by having received Lodovico who has brought a letter from the Venetian Senate and who is also her kinsman. The entire incident and her precedence is a threat to Iago's plan, and he abruptly interrupts their conversation, thus demonstrating that he now has Cassio's place and rank. The situation then turns back to Iago's advantage, for Desdemona seizes the opportunity to talk about Cassio, and Othello, whose language even while accepting the letter consisted of words with normally sexual connotations—'I kiss the instrument of their pleasures' (4.1.213)—now uses *this* 'instrument' merely as a prop to cover his eavesdropping on Desdemona's and Lodovico's conversation. Finally, private passion conquers duty altogether as Othello strikes his wife in public.

DESDEMONA'S SWEET SONG

Desdemona is now naturally distraught. Their next meeting, the so-called 'brothel scene' (4.2), ends with an agonizing promise of reconciliation in which for a few moments it seems that Othello was about to accept Desdemona's protestations of innocence. His simple insult, 'Impudent strumpet' (l. 82), gives way to a progression of questions—'Are not you a strumpet?', 'What, not a whore?', 'Is 't possible?'—which seems to display an increasing uncertainty concerning her guilt. This then prompts Desdemona's plea to heaven to forgive them *both*, which is probably best delivered as a renewed attempt to stress the equality of their relationship and the truth of their mutual love. For a brief moment he seems to concur in this image of forgiveness—'I cry you mercy, then'—but this is an illusion. The admission of his mistake is merely ironical and the phase which follows is a rejection of her and everything that she has just said: 'I took you for that cunning whore of Venice / That married with Othello' (4.2.90–1). For a second time he casts her away, and for a second time he calls himself by his name 'Othello'. After he has gone, she summons Iago and asks him to mediate for her. The trumpets sound for an official dinner and he prompts her back to her public role with the promise 'all things shall be well' (4.2.172). . . .

In the next scene, as Lodovico takes his leave, Othello 'looks gentler than he did', but Desdemona, still with no clear conception of what is wrong, is haunted by the old song her mother's maid Barbary sang when her lover 'proved mad, / And did forsake her'—the 'willow song'.

The major significance of this scene is not so much that the song is sung as that it is broken off. The story of the song is too close to Desdemona's own situation to be borne, and she first muddles the order of the stanzas before finally stopping altogether, unable to go on. By this stage in the play, Desdemona is the only character who is still 'in tune'. It is vital therefore that her song should be well performed. She is an accomplished musician and must be seen to be so, otherwise the double collapse of her song is meaningless or merely embarrassing. . . .

The song has two important dramatic functions. It displays Desdemona's emotional state and manipulates the audience's response to her. In her previous conversation with Emilia she has reiterated her beliefs concerning her marriage to Othello, but the audience, who alone have the benefit of knowing exactly what is happening, may well be feeling that Emilia's worldly view is more sensible and pragmatic. The song has the effect of stripping away the accidentals in the current situation and reminding us not only of what love might be but also of the nature of Othello's and Desdemona's love before Iago set to work. It speaks directly to the hearts and minds of the audience, and has the effect of making us appreciate the absolute truth of what Desdemona represents as opposed to the worldly truth of Emilia's observations. This reaction to her is exactly the same as that which Othello has always experienced. He recognizes that she can 'sing the savageness out of a bear' and is afraid of the power of her words. He refuses to allow the rational force of words to interfere with his irrational passion. He is afraid that she will render him incapable of performing the task that he has set himself—the necessary, rightful killing of a woman who has wronged him: 'I'll not expostulate with her lest her body and beauty unprovide my mind again' (4.1.200). But it is not her body and beauty which weaken his resolve, for he comes to her while she is asleep and kisses her, exulting in her beauty but still quite firm in his intentions. The act of expostulation of course necessitates talking to her, and this he is not prepared to risk. When she wakes, he stops her expression of pity and tenderness for his overwrought state and prevents her explaining her motivations and actions. She realizes her danger, and her line 'Kill me tomorrow, let me live tonight' (5.2.84) is a last attempt to restore sanity to the situation. She knows that if only she could talk to him, all things would indeed be well; a brief moment is all that is needed, 'But half an hour. . . . But while I say one prayer' (ll.86–8). But the entire play is organized so that there is not one scene which presents the two of them talking privately together, and part of the horrific quality of the 'brothel' scene arises from the fact that he has set up the interview in order to prove her guilt and is not talking *to* her but *at* her.

WHAT MIGHT HAVE BEEN

Othello takes his revenge, only to learn immediately that it is not after all complete and that Cassio is not dead: 'Not Cassio killed? Then murder's out of tune / And sweet revenge grows harsh' (5.2.118–19). For Othello at this instant, imbued with Iago's false music, harmony could only be achieved if both adulterous lovers had died.

It is left to Emilia . . . to take over the feminine strength of the play after Desdemona's death to bring Othello to a recognition of the truth. With the dawning of understand-

---

OTHELLO'S FINAL SPEECH

OTHELLO. Soft you, a word or two before you go.
I have done the state some service, and they know't.
No more of that. I pray you, in your letters,
When you shall these unlucky deeds relate,
Speak of me as I am. Nothing extenuate,
Nor set down aught in malice. Then must you speak
Of one that loved not wisely, but too well;
Of one not easily jealous, but, being wrought,
Perplexed in the extreme; of one whose hand,
Like the base Judean, threw a pearl away
Richer than all his tribe; of one whose subdued eyes,
Albeit unusèd to the melting mood,
Drops tears as fast as the Arabian trees
Their med'cinable gum. Set you down this.
And say besides that in Aleppo once,
Where a malignant and a turbaned Turk
Beat a Venetian and traduced the state,
I took by th' throat the circumcised dog.
And smote him—thus. [*He stabs himself.*]

Othello 5.2.334–52, ed. Alvin Kernan. New York: New American Library, 1963, p. 163.

ing, Othello's language reverts to normal. For the first time since he came to suspect his wife he considers himself as a soldier rather than simply an aggrieved husband. Now, again, he is able to talk with some ease about the two things which were dearest to him—his profession and his love— but this time his rejection of Desdemona has been absolute and irreversible and for a third time he refers to himself in the third person: 'Man but a rush against Othello's breast, / And he retires. Where should Othello go?' (5.2.273-74), and then again some ten lines later: 'That's he that was Othello; here I am.'

The very construction of Othello's final speech serves to underline all that is lost in the tragedy. His reminder that he has done the state some service gives way to personal thoughts both of Desdemona, the 'pearl' he has thrown away, and of his own nature. These are then combined as he repeats the service to the state which he had once performed in Aleppo by killing a foreigner who had harmed a Venetian. . . .

On one level this is a vengeful triumph for Iago's white racism: the 'old black ram' has been justly punished for tupping the white ewe (1.1.90). On another, Iago, as devil has achieved his ends, for according to conventional Christian belief both of his victims are damned—she for perjuring herself in laying claim to the sin of suicide (5.1.127) and he for the double sin of murder and self-murder. But neither of these possible views can be upper-most in the audience's mind. Emilia's swan-song, the 'willow, willow' refrain, reminds the audience of Desdemona's song and the dramatic reality which it created. The fact that love is unrequited is also proof that love exists. The protagonists of the play may be dead, but for those left alive—including those members of the audience who did not hang up their brains along with their hats on entering the theatre—the possibility of love remains. The tune that Iago was calling—the declaration that love is 'merely a lust of the blood and a permission of the will' (1.3.333)—is broken not with the torture that Lodovico has ordered but by the results of what he himself has engineered. The 'tragic loading of the bed' is a positive reminder not only of what might have been, but of what might be.

The Skillful Uses of Poetry and Imagery in *Othello*

D.A. Traversi

Shakespeare's use in *Othello* of magnificent language that conjures vivid, often almost palpable images is equal to the greatest examples of poetry in any of his works. According to noted literary scholar D.A. Traversi (author of *An Approach to Shakespeare*), word images of blood, both hot and cold, appear throughout the play, tying together both characters and plot elements. References to smells and other manifestations of the senses, for example, are frequent, and images of soldiers, battles, and war also abound. Shakespeare uses these, says Traversi, to help define his characters, as when Othello characteristically spouts the poetry of war and Iago regularly dredges up word images of bestiality and animalistic urges. Imagery also heightens the realism and makes the drama more powerful. As Traversi memorably puts it, "Plot and imagery, dramatic development and poetic expression are fused" in *Othello* "as never before."

Othello is, by common consent, one of Shakespeare's most completely "objective" plays. The internal conflict of *Hamlet*, the identification of the hero's tragedy with the effort to achieve self-definition, is now polarized into the more truly dramatic conflict between Othello and Iago. The substitution as vehicles of the tragic emotion of one complex and incoherent character by two more simple, sharply defined personalities in conflict carries with it an extension of the ability to present the dramatic implications of character. . . . Hamlet unites a vast number of impulses and feelings in the

Excerpted from D.A. Traversi, *An Approach to Shakespeare* (London: Sands, 1956). Reprinted by permission of the author.

utterances of a single man, but it cannot be said that his behaviour is always consistent or his motives fully compre-
hensible. Othello, on the other hand, is fully and continu-
ously a person. His sentiments and actions are throughout
perfectly intelligible, perfectly consistent with the character
as defined; his emotions, unlike those of Hamlet, are always
strictly related to their causes as dramatically presented.
Othello is, indeed, the first of a series of Shakespearean heroes whose sufferings are explicitly related to their own failings, but who manage in spite of these failings to attain
tragic dignity. . . . He dramatizes as "nobility" his own incapacity to cope with life; and . . . the very weakness which is
obvious to all around him and by which Iago engineers his
downfall is turned into true tragedy. The dramatic construction of the play, in short, turns upon the close, intricate
analysis by which the two contrasted characters of the Moor
and his Ancient are at every moment dovetailed, seen as opposed but strictly related conceptions. . . .

INTENSE HEAT BENEATH A COLD SURFACE

It is obvious (and this is a convenient starting point) that the
poetry of Othello is largely concentrated upon physical passion, but the peculiar way in which that passion is habitually
expressed by him is highly significant. His poetry naturally
dwells repeatedly upon love; but the feeling it expresses is
one which, by revealing its own incompleteness, suggests an
inability to attain adequate fulfilment. In his meditation, for
instance, over the sleeping Desdemona before he stifles her
(V. ii), we find intensity remarkably matched by coldness,
sensuous feeling by a curious remoteness from the "blood."
Beginning with an invocation to "you *chaste* stars," he goes
on to speak of a skin "whiter than *snow*" and "*smooth as
monumental alabaster*"; while there is something intense
but distant in the apostrophe to "thy light," which follows,
and in the almost studied reference to "Promethean heat."
Collecting together these images, we come to feel that
Othello's passion at this critical moment is as cold on the
surface as it is intense just below; it combines a certain
monumental frigidity in expression with a tremendous impression of the activity of the senses.

That the senses are present is clearly guaranteed—at this
stage in the play—by Othello's own behaviour; and, indeed,
the same speech proves that this is so. As he gazes upon his

victim, his underlying sensuality is felt above all in the comparison of Desdemona to the rose and in the keenness with
which the sense of smell appears in "balmy breath" and in
"I'll smell it on the tree." Even here, however, the sense of incompleteness persists. The impression is one of overwhelming passion unable to express itself otherwise than in cold
and distant imagery: the imagery, never quite freed from the
conventional, of the sonnets. . . . Even when he is stressing
the full happiness he had hoped to find in his love, he
chooses to see perfection, not in terms of overflowing vitality, but in the chill flawlessness of a precious stone:

> Nay, had she been true,
> If heaven would make me such another world
> Of one entire and perfect *chrysolite*,
> I'd not have sold her for it.
>
> (5.2)

It is not, indeed, in devotion to Desdemona that Othello expresses most powerfully the full possibilities of his nature.
The strength of his passionately emotional being finds adequate expression, not in love, but in triumphant soldiership,
in his reference to the

> Pride, pomp, and circumstance of glorious war.
>
> (3.3)

Here in the poetry of action, untrammeled by reference to
objects and needs beyond itself, the egoism essential to the
character realizes itself fully and without hindrance. In
Othello's love poetry the same intensity fails to express itself
completely towards another person; it remains apparently
cold on the surface, with an intense fire beneath that makes
it the more capable of corruption.

IAGO DWELLS ON BESTIALITY

This corruption, the central theme of the play, is the work of
Iago. The image of the rose . . . implies that of the "canker"
which destroys it; the simultaneous presence of these twin
aspects of passion is here given tragic projection in a clash
of opposed attitudes. To understand fully the inadequacy of
Othello's passion and the fact that it precedes his tragedy, we
have to turn to Iago, for the two characters, as I have said, are
contrasted aspects of a single situation. At first sight the Ancient is all that his general is not, cynical and "intellectual"
where Othello is passionate and trusting to the point of folly.
These qualities, however, are not merely opposed but com-

plementary. If Othello's passion expresses itself in a peculiar coldness, Iago's cynicism and belittlement of natural emotion are full of the feeling of "blood." "Blood," or sexual emotion, is the driving force of his intelligence, although it is a force always controlled and criticized by that intelligence. He tells Desdemona on her arrival at Cyprus that he is "nothing if not critical" (II. i), and he shows Roderigo a passionate (that is the only word for it) contempt for "blood"; but it is "blood" which is at the root of the man, criticism and all. Consider the temper of his remarks to Roderigo, when he is advancing the claims of reason and control:

> If the balance of our lives had not one scale of reason to poise another of sensuality, the blood and baseness of our natures would conduct us to most preposterous conclusions; but we have reason to cool our raging motions, our carnal stings, our unbitted lusts.
>
> (1.3)

How intensely we feel "blood" at work in the very criticism of passion! "Reason" balances—"poises," as Shakespeare so delicately puts it—the scale of sensuality, foreseeing in its unchecked operation the "most preposterous conclusions"; but the vigour of the references to "raging motions," "carnal stings," and "unbitted lusts" demonstrates unmistakably the source of Iago's peculiar vitality in action. . . . Iago's intellect dwells from the first pungently, insistently, upon the bestiality which underlies human passion; but the presence of the despised emotions is implied in the very intensity with which they are contemplated. It is impossible not to feel the intense sexuality behind his feverish activity in the dark at the opening of the play. Revealing itself in the persistent animality with which he incites Roderigo to disturb the "fertile climate" in which Othello dwells and so to "poison his delight," it dominates both the man and the scene [in which Iago calls to Brabantio]:

> Even now, now, very now, an old black ram
> Is tupping your white ewe. Arise, arise;
> Awake the snorting citizens with the bell,
> Or else the devil will make a grandsire of you.
>
> (1.1)

The grotesque tone of the last lines in itself reflects the source of the intensity behind Iago's every action. The "passionate" Othello never expresses himself in love with such physical intensity as the sceptical, controlled Iago; in this paradox lies a key to the whole play.

THE POISON BECOMES ACTIVE

It is Shakespeare's achievement to have converted into a tragedy this intuition of opposed emotions simultaneously present in a single situation. Othello and Iago, for the duration of their tragedy, live the conflict active in Shakespeare's imagination. If Iago represents the "canker" in the "rose" of Othello's love, we must watch that canker gaining ground step by step in the development of the intrigue. . . . Othello, the tragic hero in his weakness and nobility, stands at the centre of the play. In his self-imposed consistency he is the point upon which the whole action turns; the forces which dissolve his integrity operate through the hostility of Iago by bringing to the surface his own deficiencies. The fusion of dramatic purpose and poetic impulse sought by Shakespeare in the self-defining complexities of the problem plays

SYMBOLS OF UNIVERSAL FORCES

Shakespeare uses imagery in Othello *in the form of symbols, as briefly explained here by former Yale University scholar Alvin Kernan.*

Othello offers a variety of interrelated symbols that locate and define in historical, natural, social, moral, and human terms those qualities of being and universal forces that are forever at war in the universe and between which tragic man is always in movement. On one side there are Turks, cannibals, barbarism, monstrous deformities of nature, the brute force of the sea, riot, mobs, darkness, Iago, hatred, lust, concern for the self only, and cynicism. On the other side there are Venice, *The City*, law, senates, amity, hierarchy, Desdemona, love, concern for others, and innocent trust. As the characters of the play act and speak, they bring together, by means of parallelism and metaphor, the various forms of the different ways of life. There is, for example, a meaningful similarity in the underhanded way Iago works and the ruse by which the Turks try to fool the Venetians into thinking they are bound for Rhodes when their object is Cyprus. Or, there is again a flash of identification when we hear that the reefs and shoals that threaten ships are "ensteeped," that is, hidden under the surface of the sea, as Iago is hidden under the surface of his "honesty."

Alvin Kernan, ed., *Introduction to* Othello. New York: New American Library, 1963, p. xxxii.

is at last achieved in the full objectivity of his first completely realized and in some ways most disquieting tragedy. . . .

If Othello's "nobility" provides one of the main conceptions upon which the closely knit structure of the play rests, the "critical" scepticism of Iago is certainly the other. Through his plotting, the mysterious poison which had worked, according to Brabantio, upon Desdemona becomes an active and sinister reality. For Iago *is* that poison, no longer hinted at or obscurely present in minds never fully conscious of it, but turned to destructive activity. According to his "philosophy," there is nothing in the world of "nature" to prevent desire from passing easily—and meaninglessly—from one object to another. In the case of Desdemona he contends that it must so pass. . . .

Love, being merely a prompting of the senses to which the will gives assent, needs to be continually "inflamed" if the blood itself is not to be "made dull with the act of sport." For love . . . is simply an "appetite," intense but impermanent, like all sensual experience, and in particular like the impressions of taste. In the moment of fulfilment, Iago tells us, it is full of relish, of "delicate tenderness"; but it must continually be "fed," lest it turn to abhorrence, "disrelish" and "heave the gorge" in nausea at the former object of its choice. The original impulse, once satisfied, fatally demands renewal; without this, it turns to indifference and even to loathing. In this way the doubts and reservations that from the first accompany Othello's love in the minds of those who surround him are given clear logical expression. Brabantio had thought that Desdemona's choice of Othello, because prompted by irrational passion, was against the rules of nature; Iago, on the contrary, believes not only that the choice was natural but that "nature," which had brought her to it, would inevitably drive her to change. It is the conflict between this attitude, at once rational and essentially destructive, and Othello's generous but uncritical acceptance of the promptings of passion that is the subject of the play. . . .

JEALOUSY CREEPS INTO OTHELLO'S MIND

The transition from concord and fulfilment to passion-driven strife is handled by Shakespeare with considerable care. In the following scenes (II. ii, iii) the motives of felicity and disillusionment are simultaneously developed. It is night, the night in which Othello has announced "the celebration of his nuptial," but also the night in which Iago's activity turns rejoicing into savagery and drunkenness. His instrument to this end is Cassio, in whom all his unflattering conclusions with regard to love find their confirmation. We shall only understand Iago's part in this tragedy if we realize that he plays throughout upon the real weaknesses of his victims. These weaknesses he elevates, following his "philosophy," into consistent principles, turning what is largely infirmity, susceptibility, or indecision into a positive tendency to evil; but his observations, though they do not account fully for the behaviour of his victims, always pick on something really vulnerable in them. And that something is invariably connected with desire or "appetite." Cassio's imagination, stirred by Iago, lingers upon Desdemona with intense but passing sensuality. She is "exquisite," "a fresh and delicate creature," with an "inviting" though "right modest eye." He regards her, in short, as a choice morsel to be contemplated, tasted, and enjoyed, so Iago, in speaking of "provocation" and "an alarum to love" (II. iii), simply gives substance to an innermost thought. For Iago merely brings consistency to unrealized desires, which thereby become in his hands instruments all the more dangerous for being imperfectly understood by his victims. Having observed in Cassio just sufficient "loose affections" to make his accusations plausible, he uses him to bring out Othello's unconsidered sensuality, to ruin his judgement and destroy his peace.

By inflaming the fuddled Cassio to act, Iago releases the forces of passion on the island. As the drunken revelry, prevailing, takes the mind prisoner, so jealousy creeps into Othello's mind through Iago's action upon the instability which makes his will—unknown to himself—the slave of passion. Othello, as we have seen, has neglected the part played by physical desire in his "free and bounteous" love for Desdemona; Iago, for whom all love is simply the reaching-out of such desire for gratification, gives a very different interpretation of the Moor's character:

His soul is so enfetter'd to her love,
That she may make, unmake, do what she list,
Even as her appetite shall play the god
With his weak function.

(2.3)

It was precisely this idea of being "enfettered" by his love that Othello had so confidently rejected in asking permis-

sion to bring Desdemona to Cyprus (I. iii); it offended his belief in himself as a warrior and as a man. But Iago's action,
based as always on the rationalization of affection as "appetite," aims directly at the dissolution of this heroic simplicity and at subduing Othello by bringing out the animal
beneath.

In this he succeeds with surprising ease: surprising, that
is, unless we remember how Shakespeare has prepared the
way by stressing the Moor's disastrous ingenuousness. Iago
knows that his victim, once confused, is lost, so his primary
aim is to involve him in uncertainty. For Othello is quite incapable of suspending judgement. Suspense offends his self-
confidence, contrasts with the capacity for action upon
which he prides himself. His nature demands an immediate
resolution, which can in practice be nothing but an acceptance of Iago's insinuations:

> . . . to be once in doubt
> Is once to be resolved; exchange me for a goat,
> When I shall turn the business of my soul
> To such exsufflicate and blown surmises,
> Matching thy inference. . . .

                                              (3.3)

A Slavery of Passion

Flattering his victim's "free and open nature," Iago proceeds
to clip the wings of his freedom and to convert his frankness
into suspicion. Having first deprived him of certainty, he
plays upon his sensual fancy, describes Cassio's "dream"
with a full insistence upon the grossness of physical contacts, and makes him visualize the sin by which Desdemona
is offending his self-esteem. . . .

The increasing insolence—one can call it nothing else—
of Iago's comments as he comes to realize that his success is
assured is most notable. Perhaps, the irony reaches its climax when the plotter makes his victim stand aside and as-
sist in silence at what he imagines to be Cassio's account of
Desdemona's infidelity. Every word is a mortal wound for
Othello's pride. Iago sneers, and disclaims the sneer with a
phrase that is itself an affirmation of contempt:

OTHELLO. Dost thou mock me?

IAGO.   I mock you! no, by heaven,
     Would you would bear your fortune *like a man.*

He roundly taxes the heroic Othello with lack of manliness:

Whilst you were here o'erwhelmed with your grief—
A passion most unsuiting such a man—
Cassio came hither. . .

                         Marry, patience;
Or I shall say you are all in all in spleen,
And nothing of a man.

                                        (4.1)

Nothing could do more than this savage element of caricature in Iago's treatment of Othello to convey the degradation
of the victim. . . .

A few ambiguous phrases, a trick almost infantile in its
simplicity, and a persistent inflaming of the sensual imagination of his victim, and Iago has reduced Othello to an absolute slavery to passion. He himself, in a solitary moment,
describes perfectly his own method and achievement:

The Moor already changes with my poison:
Dangerous conceits are in their nature poisons:
Which at the first are scarce found to distaste,
But with a little act upon the blood,
Burn like the mines of sulphur.

                                        (3.3)

The relation of poison to taste, and of both to the action of
the "blood," is by now familiar. It describes the process
which has reduced Othello's egoism to incoherence. He now
sees himself, in his imagination, betrayed; and it is the
knowledge, rather than the betrayal, which affects him:

I had been happy, if the general camp,
Pioneers and all, had tasted her sweet body,
So I had nothing known.

                                        (3.3)

The form of this confession is highly revealing. The problem
of *Othello* is the problem of consciousness, of the relationship of instinctive life to critical detachment. It is precisely
because knowledge, reason, is in *Othello* a destructive fac-
ulty at war with heroic simplicity that the tragedy takes
place. By the end of this scene Othello's new "knowledge"
has had two consequences. It has destroyed the simplicity
upon which his real nobility had been based, and it has
roused his own sensual impulses to a destructive fury. . . .

OTHELLO'S SURRENDER TO BESTIALITY

The scene in which these developments take place forms a
kind of pivot upon which the whole subsequent action turns.

At the end of it Othello's fate is sealed, and we have only to trace the growth in him of destructive animal feeling and the crumbling into futility of his personal pride. As it closes, Othello abjures love and invokes vengeance in a speech which reveals the changing temper of his emotions:

> Like to the Pontic sea,
> Whose icy current and compulsive course
> Ne'er feels retiring ebb, but keeps due on
> To the Propontic and the Hellespont;
> Even so my bloody thoughts, with violent pace,
> Shall ne'er look back, ne'er ebb to humble love,
> Till that a capable and wide revenge
> Swallow them up. Now, by yond marble heaven,
> In the due reverence of a sacred vow,
> I here engage my words.

(3.3)

. . . As the plot advances, and Iago's control over Othello grows, the element of "blood," which had been lacking in his expressions of love, makes a disturbing appearance—disturbing, because it does not come to give warmth and embodiment to passion, but rather appears as an acute and terrible repulsion against all contacts of the body. We see and feel its effects when he falls into a fit and mumbles frenziedly, in the presence of the mocking and exultant Iago, about "noses, ears, and lips!" (IV. i) We feel them in those bestial phrases in which his outraged egoism gropes towards its revenge: "I'll tear her all to pieces" (III. iii); "I see that nose of yours, but not that dog I shall throw it to" (IV. i); and still more in the combination of affronted self-respect and rising savagery which prompts the exclamation, "I will chop her into messes; cuckold me!" (IV. i) But they appear most clearly of all, and in closer relation to the love they are corroding, in that terrible scene (IV. ii) in which the crazed Othello turns, with a mixture of intense physical attraction and open repulsion, upon Desdemona. . . . Desdemona is a "*rose*-lipp'd cherubin"—such imagery, a compound of poetic convention and deep emotion, is very characteristic—and Othello's loathing is expressed in typical sense imagery:

> DESDEMONA. I hope my noble lord esteems me honest.
> OTHELLO. O, ay; as summer flies are in the shambles,
> That quicken even with blowing. O thou weed,
> Who art so lovely fair and smell'st so sweet
> That the sense aches at thee, would thou had'st ne'er been
> born.

(4.2)

. . . *Othello* is precisely a dramatic representation of the in-evitable degeneration, in a world where "value" has no foundation, of desire into selfish and destructive appetite. This surrender to bestiality brings with it the collapse of Othello's integrity as a person. He expresses himself, as I have suggested, most confidently in the egoistic poetry of war; and it is significant that his acceptance of Iago's insinu-ations is regarded by him as tantamount to a renunciation of his prowess as a soldier. As his ruin proceeds, the egoism which had always been a part of his character comes more and more to the fore, not in connection with military glory, but rather in his attitude towards his own folly. In the last scene this folly is completely unmasked. Emilia addresses him as "dull Moor," and his own comment is as simple as it is true—"O fool, fool, fool!" Yet, in spite of all his folly, his egoism contains a considerable degree of tragic dignity. The weakness and the tragedy stand, in fact, in the closest rela-tionship. The great speeches in which he attains tragic stature by expressing his "nobility," are, at the same time, merciless exposures of weakness. In the first of them, made to Desdemona, what emerges above all is the unprepared-ness of the speaker to meet the situation in which he finds himself. Had life presented to Othello a problem which could have been met by the active creation of a nobility at once true and flattering to his self-esteem, all—we are told—would have been well.

> Had it pleased heaven
>   To try me with affliction,

he begins, and in cataloguing the forms which that affliction might have taken we feel the speaker recovering confidence, assuring himself that in resistance too there is a kind of heroism, that the exercise of patience to the limit of en-durance is not incompatible with his conception of his own moral dignity. It is only in the latter part of the speech that we are shown the true source of Othello's suffering:

> . . . but, alas, to make me
> A fixed figure for the time of scorn
> To point his slow, unmoving finger at!
>
>   (4.2)

To become an object of ridicule without being able to react, to assert his own "nobility"—this is the shame from which Othello feels that there is no escape, and which accompanies him to his tragic end.

A FUSION OF POETRY, PLOT, AND IMAGERY

I have attempted by analysis to bring out the advance in Shakespeare's dramatic power represented by *Othello*. His control of the intrigue is far more complete than it had ever been in the problem plays. In *Hamlet* and *Measure for Measure* plot and poetry are still comparatively separate entities; Hamlet's soliloquies are imperfectly fused with the rather disjointed action of the play, and the Duke's function vacillates between the engineering of the plot and the resolution of its problems in terms of poetic "symbolism." *Othello* is very different. The process by which Iago undermines Othello's confidence is perfectly reflected in the corrupting entry of his cynical, destructive "blood" imagery into his victim's noble but self-contained poetry. Plot and imagery, dramatic development and poetic expression are fused as never before. . . . But, in spite of all the interrelation of imagery, Iago is felt to be definitely opposed to Othello in the dramatic scheme. In spite of all his shortcomings, Othello is felt to be connected with love and natural emotion; and there is nothing grudging about the nobility which Shakespeare confers upon him at his best moments. Iago, on the other hand, is felt, for all his superior "intelligence," to be at once limited and evil; in fact, he is Shakespeare's personal development of the conventional Machiavellian villain of the stage. Within the unity still (as always) imposed by related imagery and by a closely continued dramatic scheme, we are for the first time within reach of the decisive orientation of Shakespearean good and evil.

CHAPTER 2

The Play's Pivotal Characters

Othello: A Noble Soul Overcome by Passion

A.C. Bradley

The following masterful essay is by the late, highly respected University of Oxford scholar A.C. Bradley,
whose lectures and writings about Shakespeare's plays
and characters continue to be widely read and quoted.
Bradley maintains that the combination of Othello's noble nature and the unfortunate predicament in which
he becomes embroiled inspires a mixture of love and
pity in the play's readers and spectators unlike that
elicited by any other major Shakespearean character.
The author rejects the often touted idea that the Moor
is a "noble savage" who reverts to his primitive nature
in the play's later scenes. Instead, in chronicling the
character's emotional changes from act to act, Bradley
emphasizes his civilized qualities, including his
sense of honor and his deep love for Desdemona,
which remains steadfast even in the act of killing her.

The character of Othello is comparatively simple, but, as I have
dwelt on the prominence of intrigue and accident in the play, it
is desirable to show how essentially the success of Iago's plot is
connected with this character. Othello's description of himself as

> one not easily jealous, but, being wrought,
> Perplexed in the extreme,

is perfectly just. His tragedy lies in this—that his whole nature was indisposed to jealousy, and yet was such that he
was unusually open to deception, and, if once wrought to
passion, likely to act with little reflection, with no delay, and
in the most decisive manner conceivable.

AS IF FROM WONDERLAND

Let me first set aside a mistaken view. I do not mean the
ridiculous notion that Othello was jealous by temperament,

Excerpted from A.C. Bradley, *Shakespearean Tragedy* (London: Macmillan, 1904).

but the idea, which has some little plausibility, that the play is primarily a study of a noble barbarian, who has become a Christian and has imbibed some of the civilisation of his employers, but who retains beneath the surface the savage passions of his Moorish blood and also the suspiciousness regarding female chastity common among Oriental peoples, and that the last three Acts depict the outburst of these original feelings through the thin crust of Venetian culture. . . . All arguments against it must end in an appeal to the reader's understanding of Shakespeare. If he thinks it is like Shakespeare to look at things in this manner; that he had a historical mind and . . . that he laboured to make his Romans perfectly Roman, to give a correct view of the Britons in the days of Lear or Cymbeline, to portray in Hamlet a stage of the moral consciousness not yet reached by the people around him, the reader will also think this interpretation of *Othello* probable. To me it appears hopelessly un-Shakespearean. . . . I do not mean that Othello's race is a matter of no account. It has, as we shall presently see, its importance in the play. It makes a difference to our idea of him; it makes a difference to the action and catastrophe. But in regard to the essentials of his character it is not important; and if anyone had told Shakespeare that no Englishman would have acted like the Moor, and had congratulated him on the accuracy of his racial psychology, I am sure he would have laughed.

Othello is, in one sense of the word, by far the most romantic figure among Shakespeare's heroes; and he is so partly from the strange life of war and adventure which he has lived from childhood. He does not belong to our world, and he seems to enter it we know not whence—almost as if from wonderland. There is something mysterious in his descent from men of royal siege; in his wanderings in vast deserts and among marvellous peoples . . . in the sudden vague glimpses we get of numberless battles and sieges in which he has played the hero and has borne a charmed life. . . .

THE GREATEST POET OF THEM ALL

And he is not merely a romantic figure; his own nature is romantic. . . . Indeed, if one recalls Othello's most famous speeches—those that begin, 'Her father loved me,' 'O now for ever,' 'Never, Iago,' 'Had it pleased Heaven,' 'It is the cause,' 'Behold, I have a weapon,' 'Soft you, a word or two before you go'—and if one places side by side with these

speeches an equal number by any other hero, one will not
doubt that Othello is the greatest poet of them all. There is
the same poetry in his casual phrases—like 'These nine
moons wasted,' 'Keep up your bright swords, for the dew
will rust them,' 'You chaste stars,' 'It is a sword of Spain, the
ice-brook's temper,' 'It is the very error of the moon'—and in
those brief expressions of intense feeling which ever since
have been taken as the absolute expression, like

> If it were now to die,
> 'Twere now to be most happy; for, I fear,
> My soul hath her content so absolute
> That not another comfort like to this
> Succeeds in unknown fate,

or

> If she be false, O then Heaven mocks itself,
> I'll not believe it;

or

> No, my heart is turned to stone; I strike it, and it hurts my
> hand. . . .

And this imagination, we feel, has accompanied his whole
life. He has watched with a poet's eye the Arabian trees drop-
ping their med'cinable gum, and the Indian throwing away
his chance-found pearl; and has gazed in a fascinated dream
at the Pontic sea rushing, never to return, to the Propontic
and the Hellespont; and has felt as no other man ever felt
(for he speaks of it as none other ever did) the poetry of the
pride, pomp, and circumstance of glorious war.

So he comes before us, dark and grand, with a light upon
him from the sun where he was born; but no longer young,
and now grave, self-controlled, steeled by the experience of
countless perils, hardships and vicissitudes, at once simple
and stately in bearing and in speech, a great man naturally
modest but fully conscious of his worth, proud of his services
to the state, unawed by dignitaries and unelated by honours,
secure, it would seem, against all dangers from without and
all rebellion from within. And he comes to have his life
crowned with the final glory of love, a love as strange, adventurous and romantic as any passage of his eventful history,
filling his heart with tenderness and his imagination with ecstasy. For there is no love, not that of Romeo in his youth,
more steeped in imagination than Othello's.

The sources of danger in this character are revealed but
too clearly by the story. In the first place, Othello's mind, for

all its poetry, is very simple. He is not observant. His nature tends outward. He is quite free from introspection, and is not given to reflection. Emotion excites his imagination, but it confuses and dulls his intellect. . . . In the second place, for all his dignity and massive calm (and he has greater dignity than any other of Shakespeare's men), he is by nature full of the most vehement passion. . . . This, and other aspects of his character, are best exhibited by a single line—one of Shakespeare's miracles—the words by which Othello silences in a moment the night-brawl between his attendants and those of Brabantio:

Keep up your bright swords, for the dew will rust them. . . .

MINGLED LOVE AND PITY

Lastly, Othello's nature is all of one piece. His trust, where he trusts, is absolute. Hesitation is almost impossible to him. He is extremely self-reliant, and decides and acts instantaneously. If stirred to indignation, as 'in Aleppo once,' he answers with one lightning stroke. Love, if he loves, must be to him the heaven where either he must live or bear no life. If such a passion as jealousy seizes him, it will swell into a well-nigh incontrollable flood. He will press for immediate conviction or immediate relief. Convinced, he will act with the authority of a judge and the swiftness of a man in mortal pain. Undeceived, he will do like execution on himself.

This character is so noble, Othello's feelings and actions follow so inevitably from it and from the forces brought to bear on it, and his sufferings are so heart-rending, that he stirs, I believe, in most readers a passion of mingled love and pity which they feel for no other hero in Shakespeare . . . . Yet there are some critics and not a few readers who cherish a grudge against him. . . . They consider that he *was* 'easily jealous'; they seem to think that it was inexcusable in him to feel any suspicion of his wife at all; and they blame him for never suspecting Iago or asking him for evidence. I refer to this attitude of mind chiefly in order to draw attention to certain points in the story. . . .

(1) Othello, we have seen, was trustful, and thorough in his trust. He put entire confidence in the honesty of Iago, who had not only been his companion in arms, but, as he believed, had just proved his faithfulness in the matter of the marriage. This confidence was misplaced, and we happen to know it; but it was no sign of stupidity in Othello. For his

opinion of Iago was the opinion of practically everyone who knew him: and that opinion was that Iago was before all things 'honest,' his very faults being those of excess in honesty. . . .

(2) Iago does not bring these warnings to a husband who had lived with a wife for months and years and knew her like his sister or his bosom-friend. Nor is there any ground in Othello's character for supposing that, if he had been such a man, he would have felt and acted as he does in the play. But he was newly married; in the circumstances he cannot have known much of Desdemona before his marriage. . . .

(3) This consciousness in any imaginative man is enough, in such circumstances, to destroy his confidence in his powers of perception. In Othello's case, after a long and most artful preparation, there now comes, to reinforce its effect, the suggestions that he is not an Italian, nor even a European; that he is totally ignorant of the thoughts and the customary morality of Venetian women; that he had himself seen in Desdemona's deception of her father how perfect an actress she could be. As he listens in horror, for a moment at least the past is revealed to him in a new and dreadful light, and the ground seems to sink under his feet. These suggestions are followed by a tentative but hideous and humiliating insinuation of what his honest and much-experienced friend fears may be the true explanation of Desdemona's rejection of acceptable suitors, and of her strange, and naturally temporary, preference for a black man. . . .

THE WRECK OF FAITH AND LOVE

Now . . . *any* man situated as Othello was would have been disturbed by Iago's communications, and I add that many men would have been made wildly jealous. But up to this point, where Iago is dismissed, Othello, I must maintain, does not show jealousy. His confidence is shaken, he is confused and deeply troubled, he feels even horror; but he is not yet jealous in the proper sense of that word. In his soliloquy (III. iii. 258 ff.) the beginning of this passion may be traced; but it is only after an interval of solitude, when he has had time to dwell on the idea presented to him, and especially after statements of fact, not mere general grounds of suspicion, are offered, that the passion lays hold of him. Even then, however, and indeed to the very end, he is quite unlike the essentially jealous man. . . . No doubt the thought of another man's possessing the woman he loves is intolerable to him; no doubt the sense of insult and the impulse of revenge are at times most violent; and these are the feelings of jealousy proper. But these are not the chief or the deepest source of Othello's suffering. It is the wreck of his faith and his love. It is the feeling,

> If she be false, oh then Heaven mocks itself;

the feeling,

> O Iago, the pity of it, Iago!

the feeling,

> But there where I have garner'd up my heart,
> Where either I must live, or bear no life;
> The fountain from the which my current runs,
> Or else dries up—to be discarded thence. . . .

Up to this point, it appears to me, there is not a syllable to be said against Othello. But the play is a tragedy, and from this point we may abandon the ungrateful and undramatic task of awarding praise and blame. When Othello, after a brief interval, re-enters (III. iii. 330), we see at once that the poison has been at work, and 'burns like the mines of sulphur.' . . . He is 'on the rack,' in an agony so unbearable that he cannot endure the sight of Iago. . . . But he has not abandoned hope. The bare possibility that his friend is deliberately deceiving him—though such a deception would be a thing so monstrously wicked that he can hardly conceive it credible—is a kind of hope. He furiously demands proof, ocular proof. And when he is compelled to see that he is demanding an impossibility he still demands evidence. He forces it from the unwilling witness, and hears the maddening tale of Cassio's dream. It is enough. And if it were not enough, has he not sometimes seen a handkerchief spotted with strawberries in his wife's hand? Yes, it was his first gift to her.

> I know not that; but such a handkerchief—
> I am sure it was your wife's—did I to-day
> See Cassio wipe his beard with.

'If it be that,' he answers—but what need to test the fact? The 'madness of revenge' is in his blood, and hesitation is a thing he never knew. He passes judgment, and controls himself only to make his sentence a solemn vow.

A THIRST FOR REVENGE

The Othello of the Fourth Act is Othello in his fall. His fall is never complete, but he is much changed. Towards the close of the Temptation-scene [III. iii.] he becomes at times most terrible, but his grandeur remains almost undiminished. Even in the following scene (III. iv.), where he goes to test Desdemona in the matter of the handkerchief, and receives a fatal confirmation of her guilt, our sympathy with him is hardly touched by any feeling of humiliation. But in the Fourth Act 'Chaos has come.' A slight interval of time may be admitted here. It is but slight. . . . And when Othello reappears we see at a glance that he is a changed man. He is physically exhausted, and his mind is dazed. He sees everything blurred through a mist of blood and tears. . . . He mutters disjointed words; a blackness suddenly intervenes between his eyes and the world; he takes it for the shuddering testimony of nature to the horror he has just heard, and he falls senseless to the ground. When he recovers it is to watch Cassio, as he imagines, laughing over his shame. . . . The sight only adds to the confusion of intellect the madness of rage; and a ravenous thirst for revenge, contending with motions of infinite longing and regret, conquers them. The delay till night-fall is torture to him. His self-control has wholly deserted him, and he strikes his wife in the presence of the Venetian envoy. He is so lost to all sense of reality that he never asks himself what will follow the deaths of Cassio and his wife. . . .

NOT IN HATE, BUT IN HONOR

But before the end there is again a change. The supposed death of Cassio (V. i.) satiates the thirst for vengeance. The Othello who enters the bed-chamber with the words,

> It is the cause, it is the cause, my soul,

is not the man of the Fourth Act. The deed he is bound to do is no murder, but a sacrifice. He is to save Desdemona from herself, not in hate but in honour; in honour, and also in love. His anger has passed; a boundless sorrow has taken its place; and

> this sorrow's heavenly:
> It strikes where it doth love.

Even when, at the sight of her apparent obduracy [stubbornness], and at the hearing of words which by a crowning fatality can only reconvince him of her guilt, these feelings give way to others, it is to righteous indignation they give way, not to rage. . . . Pity itself vanishes, and love and admiration alone remain, in the majestic dignity and sovereign ascendancy of the close. Chaos has come and gone; and the Othello of the Council-chamber and the quay of Cyprus has returned, or a greater and nobler Othello still. As he speaks those final words in which all the glory and agony of his life—long ago in India and Arabia and Aleppo, and afterwards in Venice, and now in Cyprus—seem to pass before us, like the pictures that flash before the eyes of a drowning man, a triumphant scorn for the fetters of the flesh and the littleness of all the lives that must survive him sweeps our grief away, and when he dies upon a kiss the most painful of all tragedies leaves us for the moment free from pain, and exulting in the power of 'love and man's unconquerable mind.'

Iago the Poisoner

George W. Williams

Iago, one of the best-written villains in English literature, constitutes the corrupting force that destroys
the harmony of Othello's life and thereby creates the
conflict that drives the play's plot. This intriguing
analysis of Iago's character, by the distinguished
Duke University scholar George W. Williams, focuses
on the villain's use of poison to achieve his evil ends.
Iago pours poison in Othello's ear, says Williams, but
not the conventional liquid kind; rather, the damage
is done by a "flow of poisonous words." Williams
also dissects Iago's "animalistic" speech and thought,
with which several other characters eventually become infected.

Othello is Shakespeare's most economically constructed play.
It is spare, it is lean. It has a wonderful concentration in mat-
ters of time, space, and action; and, to be specific, it has fewer
characters of name than does any of the other tragedies.

It moves speedily and relentlessly—after the first act
which is a kind of prologue—in the confinement of an island
fortress from which there is no escape. There the marriage
of Desdemona and Othello is set against that of Emilia and
Iago and against the affair of Bianca and Cassio—a sextet of
characters bound in one way or another by sex. To these
three men, each of whom loves Desdemona in his own way,
we add Roderigo, another lover, and a few minor figures,
and we have the cast of characters of this tense play.

A MAN OF INSATIABLE FURY

In these few pages we have space only for Iago, the most en-
ergetic of the number, and because of that energy, to Shakespeare perhaps, the most interesting. Of his part in the web
of contrivance the play asks two questions: "Will you," asks
Othello at the end of the play "demand [of Iago] that demi-

Reprinted from "Iago the Poisoner," by George W. Williams, unpublished paper, 1999,
by permission. Copyright © 1999 by George W. Williams.

devil / Why he hath thus ensnared my soul and body?" And Iago asks at the beginning of the play: "To get [Cassio's] place, and to plume up my will / In double knavery—How, how?" Let us pluck out the mystery of that *why* and that *how*.

To begin before the beginning, the play tells us very little of Iago's life or personality before the opening of the story, but it appears that he is and has been always an entirely reliable and trustworthy person. A comrade in arms who could be depended on in battle and someone who could be respected for his honesty and integrity in time of peace. He was blunt and forthright, but he was truthful—always a direct, outspoken, but honest companion. There is no hint of any psychological unbalance in his nature. He had friends in high places ("three great ones") and was on good terms with his fellow soldiers; Desdemona respected him and turned to him in time of trouble, called him her "good friend." If he harbored feelings of jealousy or hatred, he kept them concealed.

But at the beginning of the play, we see a man of insatiable fury. With Iago we may ask *why* this change so complete has occurred so suddenly. Two events, two changes have taken place in the world around Iago. The first of these is the lack of promotion; the second is the marriage of Othello and Desdemona. These events are totally unconnected, and the second, indeed, should have been of no concern to Iago. But they have occurred simultaneously, and that conjunction has undone him and his even temper. The lack of promotion has confronted him with a judgement of inadequacy in his profession; the marriage has confronted him with a standard of perfect love which has shown him the inadequacy of his own marriage and, beyond that, of his own personal spirit. He comes finally to recognize that second inadequacy at the end of the play. Honest Iago tells us honestly in an aside: Cassio "hath a daily beauty in his life / That makes me ugly." It is difficult to know what precisely Iago's ugliness is, but the beauty of Cassio's spirit shows itself fully in his understanding of the character of Desdemona. He sees her as surrounded by the "grace of heaven"; and the ability to see that quality in her character is what in large part defines his own character. We may say that that is his beauty. The contrast between the two men is most specifically shown in the descriptions of Desdemona by Cassio and the ugly responses of Iago in the sequence just before Cassio becomes a victim to Iago's machinations.

HIS CIRCLE OF SILENCE

So Iago's first response to the two events is double: it addresses both of them. "To get [Cassio's] place and to plume up my will / In double knavery." Getting Cassio's place is straightforward—easily understood, and as easily accomplished. It is accomplished before the mid point of the play, where Othello says, "Now art thou my lieutenant." We might suppose that here the play was at its end; but it is not: the other half of the double knavery must work itself out. "Pluming up my will" is not so easily defined. Editors tell us that "plume" signifies the feather of a bird, and "pluming up" means adding wings to the will so that it will fly. In this play,

---

IAGO PLANS TO "ABUSE" OTHELLO'S EAR

In this soliloquy at the end of act 1, Iago speaks not only of "pluming up his will," or as George Williams says, gaining command, but also of "abusing" the Moor's ears, a reference to his poisonous speech.

IAGO. Thus do I ever make my fool my purse;
For I mine own gained knowledge should profane
If I would time expend with such snipe
But for my sport and profit. I hate the Moor,
And it is thought abroad that 'twixt my sheets
H'as done my office. I know not if't be true,
But I, for mere suspicion in that kind,
Will do, as if for surety. He holds me well;
The better shall my purpose work on him.
Cassio's a proper man. Let me see now:
To get his place, and to plume up my will
In double knavery. How? How? Let's see.
After some time, to abuse Othello's ears
That he is too familiar with his wife.
He hath a person and a smooth dispose
To be suspected—framed to make women false.
The Moor is of a free and open nature
That thinks men honest that but seem to be so;
And will as tenderly be led by th' nose
As asses are.
I have't! It is engendered! Hell and night
Must bring this monstrous birth to the world's light.
[*Exit.*]

Othello 1.3.374–95, ed. Alvin Kernan. New York: New American Library, 1963, pp. 63–64.

I think it means more and other than that also; in military terms, the plume is the ornamental headdress worn by commanding officers. Iago wants to wear symbolically such a headdress; he wants to command, he wants to be first. He wants by his will and his wit to lord it over his superiors, to command those who now command him. He brilliantly succeeds. Up to a point. And then those two most inferior to him, Emilia and Roderigo, reveal his conniving nature—unsuspected, unimagined by his superiors—and he collapses.

Iago can come no closer to explaining his jealous malice, envy, and hatred to Othello than in his recognition of his own ugliness, and he will at the end of the play say no more. He will say no more because he can say no more why this has happened to him; he is unable to define his character further. But within that circle of silence we are at the heart of his mystery.

POISON TO ACCOMPLISH HIS ENDS

Though he can not tell us *why*, he can tell us *how* if we watch him. He goes immediately to work. In the first scene, having told us he hates the Moor, he begins Othello's destruction by awakening Brabantio. Or, rather, he directs someone else to awaken Brabantio: he gets someone else to do his dirty work.

> Call up her father,
> Rouse him. Make after him, poison his delight,
> Proclaim him in the streets.

> (1.1.66–68)

Five imperatives, it will be noted, of which one is a metaphor: "poison his delight." Iago is a poisoner, he will use poison to accomplish his ends.

In *Hamlet*, the tragedy immediately preceding *Othello* in Shakespeare's development, old King Hamlet is murdered by poison which is poured into his ear. In *Othello* that literal technique of destructive poisoning is transformed into a figurative, or metaphoric, technique; what is poured into the ear is not a poisonous liquid but a flow of poisonous words. One of the Senators asks Othello if he did "poison" Desdemona's affections, but Othello is not a poisoner. Othello later suggests indeed that he might destroy Desdemona by poisoning her, but Iago prohibits that course of vengeance, suggesting the more appropriate method of death by strangulation in "the bed she hath contaminated." Iago reserves poisoning for himself.

Brabantio charges Othello with another vicious action; he claims that Othello "abused" his daughter by magic spells and charms. But he is mistaken; Othello is not an abuser: he has won his wife by telling her stories which she would "with a greedy ear / Devour up." Othello's discourse is not the malevolent power that Brabantio claims it has been, but Iago knows that he can "abuse" Othello's ears with his discourse and that it can be a fatal as well as a powerful poison.

IAGO'S REFERENCES TO ANIMALS

The precise nature of the poison in Iago's discourse can easily be demonstrated: his language is filled with allusions to animals. In the first act of the play there are fifteen allusions to animals, all of them from the mouth of Iago. Of twelve different speakers in that act of 678 lines only Iago mentions animals. It is a characteristic of Shakespeare's plays that the habit of mentioning animals to show contempt of other characters is a habit that demeans the speaker more than the persons so described. The conspicuous uniqueness of Iago in adopting this style of language defines him as one given to animalistic thinking, and he becomes, if not bestial, at least, less human. This psycho-linguistic trick continues in the second act. Iago speaks nine references to animals before 2.3.265, at which point, for the first time in the play, another character speaks an animal reference. And this is Cassio, now drunk with another kind of poison, who having lost his reputation under the direction of Iago has become "bestial." Having heard Iago's nine references, Cassio uses three more. And then, under the influence of Iago's poison, Roderigo calls himself a dog.

In the dialogue of the play, Cassio and Roderigo have both heard the series of animal references from Iago's mouth and they have both become so far contaminated by his poisoned speech in their ears that they have begun to adopt his language. Othello has heard none of the 28 references so far uttered on stage, but the spirit of Iago's suggestive language has infected even him, and in the opening scene of act three he speaks three such references (the first of the act)—"goat, haggard, toad." After these utterances, Iago smugly, but accurately, boasts:

The Moor already changes with my poison.

(3.3.325)

It is a characteristic of Shakespeare's plays that when two characters use the same words they are thinking the same thoughts. And when two characters think in the same way, they are likely to act in the same way. It could, of course, hardly be otherwise.

So that when we hear Othello using Iago's animal language, we must expect the worst. The transfer from Iago to Othello of language, thought, and action is brilliantly and conclusively demonstrated by the repetition of Iago's phrase

as prime as goats, as hot as monkeys

(4.3.403)

in Othello's mouth:

Goats and monkeys!

(4.1.256)

He utters this cry twenty lines after he has struck his wife; no other indication of the effect of Iago's poisoning is needed.

After this speech of Iago's with these animal references, Iago makes no further references to animals in the rest of the play—almost one-half of the play. Nor is there any need that he should, for Othello from 3.3 to the end of the play uses sixteen references; he is joined by Cassio, Bianca, Emilia, Roderigo, even Lodovico. Iago's poisonous language has become general.

That courteous and dignified Senator, considering the tragic bed loaded with the bodies of Desdemona, Emilia, and Othello, orders that the bed curtains be drawn because "The object poisons sight." As these deaths are the "work" of the poisoner, Lodovico's metaphor is apt. He might also have said: "the language poisons hearing," for that is Iago's work too.

The Ideal Desdemona: Aristocratic Daughter and "Fair Warrior"

Martin L. Wine

This essay, by Martin L. Wine, a professor of English at the University of Illinois, Chicago, ingeniously examines Desdemona's character by reviewing the various ways the role has been played by actresses in well-known productions of the play. Wine makes the point that in many such productions, Iago's character is allowed to dominate the action almost completely, with the result that Desdemona is often overshadowed. A sweet and loving but also strong-willed and forthright Desdemona, he says, helps to underscore the play's true tragedy—the destruction of Othello's and her love—rather than Iago's supposed victory over them.

If an overpowering Iago makes a shambles of the play that Shakespeare wrote, so does a feckless Desdemona. Altogether too many productions focus on the Othello-Iago rather than on the more significant Othello-Desdemona relationship, which is, after all, at the heart of the tragedy. Othello assumes at first that with 'proof' of Desdemona's infidelity, 'there is no more but this: / Away at once with love or jealousy!' That is melodrama. Tragedy comes to Othello when he understands clearly that he has no simple choice, for in Desdemona, as he says:

> . . . I have garnered up my heart,
> Where either I must live, or bear no life,
> The fountain from the which my current runs,
> Or else dries up. . .

To Desdemona a choice is incomprehensible; her love is absolute:

> . . . Unkindness may do much,
> And his unkindness may defeat my life,
> But never taint my love. . . .

His 'unkindness' does defeat her life, and his too. Their bond of love is their undoing, but in the end it proves stronger than all of Iago's hate. The impression of their wasted lives should haunt an audience more than the spell of Iago's 'humour' or Machiavellian cleverness. For this to happen, an audience must see in Othello what Desdemona sees in him, his 'visage in his mind'; but, equally, it must see in Desdemona what he sees in her, 'so lovely fair' and one who compels him to be 'free and bounteous to her mind'. A complete humanity, physical and spiritual, unites them. 'Let me go with him', she pleads to the Senators. His ultimate accolade to her is simply: 'my fair warrior'.

With few exceptions, in the many productions in which the Iagos dominate, the Desdemonas prove, as often as their Othellos, unexceptional. Iago's role is so actor-proof that it is probably impossible for an actor to 'ham' up the part too much. But to turn innocence and uncomprehending suffering into an active and convincing stage presence offers a tremendous challenge to an actress today. [Noted critic] Robert Brustein makes an interesting observation along these lines: 'the passive, virtuous, all-suffering Desdemona is a part that must be inhabited rather than impersonated—which may be why it is so difficult to cast in an age of women's liberation' (*New Republic*, 10 March 1982). Few actresses are able to balance child-like innocence and mature womanhood in a rounded characterisation; too often they seem either childish or so worldly intelligent that it is inconceivable that they would land themselves in this mess.

Uta Hagen's Interpretation, 1943–44

Whether the play belonged to Paul Robeson's Othello or to Jose Ferrer's Iago in the [1943] Margaret Webster production is still a subject of debate, but in that debate Uta Hagen's (Mrs Ferrer's) Desdemona figures not at all. Reviews at the time mention her in passing, but she seems to have made no impression one way or another. One reviewer summed up the prevailing attitude when he wrote that he 'could take her or leave her' (Robert Garland, *New York Journal American*, 25 May 1945).

The fault may not have been entirely Hagen's; for Webster's promptbook, now in the New York Library of the Performing Arts, indicates that the part, not all that large to begin with, was sufficiently 'cleaned up' so that only the child-like innocence of the character remained. Her banter with Iago at the beginning of the second act, before Othello arrives at Cyprus, is severely cut, including her sophisticated reference to Iago's 'alehouse humour'. Her declaration to Iago later, 'I cannot say "whore"' is also omitted, Webster not allowing her to say even that much! Also deleted is a major portion of the passage in which she blames herself for Othello's unhappy state. Iago's reference to her as being 'framed as fruitful / As the free elements' and Othello's, though not Iago's, to her being 'naked in bed' have been cut. Hagen apparently, according to the promptbook, put up a struggle on her deathbed, but the overall impression is of a 'nice' girl, with nothing of the 'fair warrior' about her. One strange bit of stage business ought perhaps to be mentioned: at the beginning of the temptation scene, when Cassio first comes to Desdemona to ask her to plead his suit with Othello, they drink mutual toasts to one another. Desdemona as perfect hostess?

DIANNE WIEST'S INTERPRETATION, 1982

'Drawling like an anxious debutante hostess trying to enliven a dreary cocktail party' is, in fact, how one reviewer described Dianne Wiest's Desdemona opposite James Earl Jones's Othello in the Broadway opening of the American Shakespeare Festival production (Stephen Harvey, *SoHo News*, 10 February 1982). He went on to say, 'she delivers a bitchy parody of frail feminine rectitude'. One or two reviewers did find Wiest 'appealing' and 'tender', but most thought that the actress, normally strong in other roles, was 'miscast' or 'a major handicap'.

From the beginning, when it opened in Connecticut the preceding summer, and throughout its lengthy pre-Broadway tour, the production ran afoul of its Desdemonas; Wiest was the third. The first Desdemona was described as 'looking like a vapid starlet on the beach at Malibu' (John Simon, *New York*, 7 September 1981), and a Chicago reviewer described the touring Desdemona as 'a corpse from the first scene' (Bury St Edmund, *Reader*, 27 November 1981). Only in the last few weeks of the Broadway run was a more convincing actress, Cecilia Hart (Mrs James Earl Jones) brought in, but by then the production had run its course. The major criticism of Wiest, as of her predecessors, was sheer inability to make Shakespearean verse come alive with feeling. Inevitably, an unbridgeable distance opened up between actress and audience, as well as, it seemed, between her and

Othello, which may partially account for what was felt to be Jones's unfelt involvement with her. Their marriage seemed implausible and the murder scene may well have been 'the most dispassionate murder of passion in stage history' (Stewart Klein, for WNEW-TV, New York, 3 February 1982). 'I am a child to chiding', says Desdemona, and Wiest seems to have taken, or had been directed to take, the reference to the 'child' Desdemona too literally, as when, in the brothel scene, after Othello's unexpectedly harsh treatment of her, she curled up on stage in a near-foetal position. At odd moments she affected a disconcerting little-girl giggle. Wiest's Desdemona was also something of a tease: at the beginning of the temptation scene, she entered carrying a rose, with which she jabbed Othello on the head and then coyly threw it to him. Klein rightly observed that 'this is not Shakespearean innocence but Rebecca of Sunnybrook Farm'. Moments like these gave the impression that every movement was calculated, not felt—in Brustein's words, 'impersonated', not 'inhabited'. Frank Rich pointed out that 'in the slapping scene, her sorrow . . . seems a bit second-hand': 'If there's not a flowing, open-hearted Desdemona to balance Iago, an Othello can't easily dramatize the hero's violent swings between the author's poles of good and evil' (*New York Times*, 4 February 1982). A Desdemona who is neither 'fair warrior' nor one for whom 'the sense aches' creates a vacuum at the centre of the tragedy which the liveliness of Iago rushes in to fill.

LISA HARROW'S INTERPRETATION, 1971–72

Youth and innocence need not mean mindlessness or foolishness as Lisa Harrow had made clear in her touchingly convincing portrayal of Desdemona to Brewster Mason's Othello for the Royal Shakespeare Company in the Stratford-London seasons of 1971–2. Playing the part with a 'child-like fragility' that Gareth Lloyd Evans, among others, found 'intensely affecting' (*Guardian*, 10 September 1971), Harrow added an unusual and interesting variation to this traditional interpretation. Remaining completely innocent herself, she nevertheless managed to impart 'an ambiguous sensuous possibility' to the role (so Garry O'Connor, *Financial Times*, 19 July 1972). Although neither Mason nor Harrow brought any sense of a deep sexual passion to their relationship, Harrow's characterisation 'for once', as Michael

Billington, writing of the London performance, indicated, 'makes Othello's suspicions seem vaguely plausible' (*Guardian*, 19 July 1972). Ian Christie said much the same thing about the earlier Stratford performance: 'Judging by the way Desdemona and Cassio flirt with each other, I am by no means certain that Othello's suspicions were unfounded' (*Daily Express*, 10 September 1971). Of course, all this makes Iago's accusations 'vaguely plausible' also; an audience rarely has this chance to see how 'evidence' from multi-sided characterisation works in *Othello*.

Furthermore, this double-edged portrayal by Harrow pointed up more directly than, say, the Jones-Wiest performances, the vulnerability at the heart of this marriage of an older man, of different race and culture, to a younger woman. On Othello's telling her about the 'magic in the web' of the lost handkerchief, Harrow's Desdemona was so innocent and guileless that she registered neither fear nor shock at first. At the mention of the 'sibyl, that had numbered in the world / The sun to course two hundred compasses', she broke into a giggle, and the tone and manner of her response—'Then would to God that I had never seen it!'—clearly indicated that she regarded his telling her this tale as some sort of joke. But just a little later, in the brothel scene, the voice of a compassionate, mature woman was to be heard. Ronald Bryden movingly describes this moment:

> Lisa Harrow's Desdemona sees his fear, and tries to gentle it, meet it with trust. In one of [director] Barton's most brilliant innovations, their fourth act confrontation ('I took you for that cunning whore of Venice') is played as a half-naked siesta together, the wife softly trying to calm her husband, make him speak, accept her caresses, and almost succeeding. I've seldom seen acting reach so near the intimate heart of marriage.
>
> (*Observer*, 12 September 1971)

Her failure to reassure her husband made the willow scene that shortly followed 'the emotional peak of the evening' (B. A. Young, *Financial Times*, 10 September 1971), and her death came close to being another. The production thus reached from time to time into 'the intimate heart' of the tragedy itself which, unfortunately, as happens so often, was undercut by an underplayed Othello and an overplayed Iago.

MAGGIE SMITH'S INTERPRETATION, 1964

An 'atmosphere of the most potent sensuality' (Bamber Gascoigne, quoted in Tynan, p. 107) was Maggie Smith's contribution to the part several years earlier opposite Laurence Olivier, in John Dexter's National Theatre production. Smith's Desdemona countered Olivier's proud, strong-willed, and highly sexed Othello with a pride, strong will, and sexual passion of her own. Here, in modern times, was the fairest warrior of them all. The strength of her many-sided characterisation gave depth and meaning to Othello's tragedy, and may be one reason that Olivier's consciously developed 'realistic' interpretation turned out to be, in the end, more 'romantic' than he and director John Dexter had intended. For once, the mutual attraction of Othello and Desdemona was both plausible and convincing. Throughout the play, Smith made evident the power that her Desdemona had over Othello, as at the beginning of the temptation scene when she never let him take his eyes off her while she pleaded the case for Cassio. Olivier, self-assured and 'egotistical' as Othello, was nevertheless completely at her mercy, almost shrivelling in weakness, when he responded that he could deny her nothing.

Bernard Levin has written that, in the final scene, Olivier's Othello 'kills with such sorrow that it is unbearable; he dies with such consciousness of waste that it is more unbearable yet' (quoted in Tynan, p. 103). Smith's Desdemona, most critics found, made credible that 'sorrow' and 'consciousness of waste'. And where Desdemona is strong and believable, Iago is diminished. At the beginning of the fourth act, Othello and Iago (Olivier and Finlay) enter together; and, as the ensign inflames the general's imagination with a verbal picture of Desdemona 'naked with her friend in bed / An hour or more', 'the two men even begin to sway gently from side to side, locked together in the rhythm of Othello's pain' (Tynan, p. 10). But the most memorable moment of this production counters this appalling scene— when Othello lifts the slain Desdemona from her deathbed and rocks back and forth with her locked in his arms. Othello's tragedy, not Iago's triumph, is what comes through, as well as Othello's triumph over Iago in that his original faith in Desdemona was warranted all along.

A few critics found Smith's Desdemona 'no more than adequate' or too much like 'an animated talking doll'. The dramatic critic of *The Times* wrote that she 'is on very distant terms with the part': 'Obviously a mettlesome girl who would not for an instant have endured domestic tyranny, she introduces facetious modern inflexions (for instance her giggling reference to "These Men" in the bedchamber scene) which clash destructively with the character' (22 April 1964). Reviewing the film made from the stage production, John Simon remarked that 'Maggie Smith's Desdemona is fine, if you like the play with two Emilias in it' (*Private Screenings*, 1967, p. 213). These last two critics were objecting apparently to a Desdemona not doll-like enough but, rather, like Emilia, a knowing woman of the world who gives as much as she gets. On the other hand, the calm dignity that Smith invested her Desdemona with at the beginning of the play and the stupified resignation that came over her later, after Othello's violent and incomprehensible treatment of her, were the emotions not of a 'doll' but of an aristocrat's daughter, whose act of marriage was as courageous as any of Othello's heroic exploits. There was a touching moment in the Senate scene when she reached out to her father to try to make him understand, and then registered sorrow when she failed. But Smith's Desdemona was immune from self-pity. Tynan describes her reaction to Othello's striking her 'across the face with the rolled-up proclamation he has received from Lodovico' in Act IV, scene I, as 'not the usual collapse into sobs; it is one of deep shame and embarrassment, for Othello's sake as well as her own. She is outraged, but tries out of loyalty not to show it' (p. 10).

As a proper Elizabethan wife, Desdemona tells her husband: 'Be as your fancies teach you. / Whate'er you be, I am obedient'. Smith's Desdemona has given up everything for Othello, but she will not relinquish her self-respect or individuality. Admittedly, Smith did not bring to the role one dimension of Desdemona that the text makes clear—the 'sweetness' that Othello sees in her, just as Olivier did not bring to Othello the grandeur and heroic nobility traditionally associated with the part. But, given their approaches, the team of Olivier and Smith meshed together as few Othellos and Desdemonas have in the stage history of the play and at least put the emphasis where it should be: on Othello *and* Desdemona.

Is Emilia Iago's Passive Accomplice?

E.A.J. Honigmann

Emilia is a pivotal character because it is she whom Iago uses to obtain the handkerchief, the "evidence" to damn Desdemona in Othello's eyes, and also she who eventually reveals the truth of Iago's treachery. Noted Shakespearean scholar and *Othello* editor E.A.J. Honigmann here examines Emilia's character, concluding that she keeps silent about the handkerchief until it is too late out of fear of her husband. This would suggest, Honigmann says, that Shakespeare considered Emilia a passive accomplice, as she appeared in the original Italian story by Giraldi Cinthio; although Honigmann emphasizes that the relationship between Iago and Emilia is much more sharply focused in Shakespeare's version.

Less complicated than her husband, Emilia is often simplified and misrepresented in the theatre. Should she be made up as middle-aged and unattractive, more or less like the Nurse in *Romeo and Juliet*? If so, one wonders why Iago married her, and the thought that Othello may be her lover (2.1.293ff.) becomes ludicrous. Iago has 'looked upon the world for four times seven years' (1.3.312–13), consequently Cinthio's account of the Ensign's wife might also apply to Emilia—'a fair and honest young woman'. She must be older than Desdemona, let us say in her mid-twenties, and definitely attractive. Hence Iago's sexual possessiveness: he may not love her, but the possibility that she has a lover 'Doth like a poisonous mineral gnaw my inwards'. Different as they are, Iago and Othello experience a similar torment, a monster of the imagination in both cases.

Cinthio's narrative throws light on a related problem, Emilia's feeling for her husband. Cinthio's 'Emilia' knew of the Ensign's plot to kill Desdemona, refused to help him, but 'did not dare, for fear of her husband, to tell her anything. She said only: "Take care not to give your husband any reason for suspicion..."'. Fear of Iago, though not expressed explicitly, explains Emilia's attitude as Shakespeare's tragedy unfolds. When they are first seen alone (3.3.304–23) his derision and her resentment prove that all is not well between them. This is a relationship more sharply focused than in Cinthio, one that proceeds quite naturally—given their characters in the play—to the wife's later defiance of her husband and his murderous revenge, both added by Shakespeare.

How guilty is Emilia of acting as a passive accomplice in Iago's plot? The question arises when Desdemona asks 'Where should I lose that handkerchief, Emilia?' and she lies, 'I know not, madam' (3.4.23–24). Just four words, yet momentous in their implications. Had she not been afraid of Iago the truth might have come out and Iago's plot would have collapsed. How typical of Shakespeare that the most passionate indictment of untruthfulness is later addressed to Emilia ('She's like a liar gone to burning hell', 5.2.127), and that Emilia then feels obliged to 'report the truth'. Her 'I know not, madam' may not

---

EMILIA REVEALS THE AWFUL TRUTH

In the following exchange in the play's climactic scene, Emilia realizes what her husband actually did with the handkerchief and reveals the truth of his evil deed to all present. Her reactions show that, though she was in a sense Iago's accomplice, she did not know of her husband's nefarious scheme until it was too late.

> OTHELLO. 'Tis pitiful; but yet Iago knows
> That she with Cassio hath the act of shame
> A thousand times committed. Cassio confessed it;
> And she did gratify his amorous works
> With that recognizance and pledge of love,
> Which I first gave her. I saw it in his hand.
> It was a handkerchief, an antique token
> My father gave my mother.
>
> EMILIA. O God! O heavenly God!
>
> IAGO. Zounds, hold your peace!
>
> EMILIA.   'Twill out, 'twill out! I peace?
> No, I will speak as liberal as the north.
> Let heaven and men and devils, let them all,
> All, all, cry shame against me, yet I'll speak.
>
> IAGO. Be wise, and get you home.

deserve to be punished in burning hell, yet what of her silence when Othello so insistently demands the handkerchief (3.4.52–99)? Shakespeare took care to have Emilia present during this painful confrontation and, hearing what she hears, she can hardly fail to understand that her lie has had serious consequences. But, being afraid, she tries to warn Desdemona without accusing Iago directly (exactly like the Ensign's wife in Cinthio)—'Is not this man jealous?' (3.4.100).

HEIGHTENING THE SUSPENSE

We must now attend to a statement thrice repeated by Emilia. Iago 'hath *a hundred times* / Wooed me to steal it [the handkerchief]'; she calls it 'That which *so often* you did bid me steal', and asks 'What will you do with't that *you have been so earnest* / *To have me filch it?*' (3.3.296–97, 313, 318–19; my italics). Shakespeare wants us to know, just before Othello makes such an issue of it in the next scene, that the handkerchief was of special interest to Iago and that Emilia had noticed this—a point repeated once more in the final scene, where it leads immediately to her death.

EMILIA.   I will not.
    [Iago draws and threatens Emilia.]

GRATIANO. Fie! Your sword upon a woman?

EMILIA. O thou dull Moor, that handkerchief thou speak'st of
    I found by fortune, and did give my husband;
    For often with a solemn earnestness—
    More than indeed belonged to such a trifle—
    He begged of me to steal't.

IAGO.   Villainous whore!

EMILIA. She give it Cassio? No, alas, I found it,
    And I did give't my husband.

IAGO.   Filth, thou liest!

EMILIA. By heaven, I do not, I do not, gentlemen.
    O murd'rous coxcomb! What should such a fool
    Do with so good a wife?

OTHELLO.   Are there no stones in heaven
    But what serves for the thunder? Precious villain!
    [The Moor runs at Iago, but is disarmed by Montano.
                Iago kills his wife.]

Othello 5.2.207–35, ed. Alvin Kernan. New York: New American Library, 1963, pp. 158–59.

For often, with a solemn earnestness
—More than indeed belonged to such a trifle—
He begged of me to steal't.
                                                (5.2.225-7)

Emilia therefore should have suspected her 'wayward husband' of being somehow connected with Othello's fury in the
handkerchief scene (3.4.51ff). And perhaps she does. Perhaps in her outburst against Desdemona's slanderer—

I will be hanged if some eternal villain . . .
Have not devised this slander, I'll be hanged else!
                                                (4.2.132-35)

—she voices her suspicion as directly as she dares. But now
the consequences would be so frightening, should her suspicion prove correct, that she takes the easy way out, accepting Iago's cool disclaimer, 'Fie, there is no such man, it
is impossible'. Emilia later refers back to this exchange, just
as Iago's guilt becomes absolutely clear.

Villainy, villainy, villainy!
I think upon't, I think I smell't, O villainy!
I thought so then: I'll kill myself for grief!
                                                (5.2.187-89)

'I thought so then': she may mean that she thought in
4.2.132ff. that some villain had slandered Desdemona, or
that she thought 'then' that Iago was responsible. The alter-
natives are to suppose either that Shakespeare wants us to
consider Emilia exceptionally dimwitted or that he made
her (like the Ensign's wife in Cinthio) too afraid of Iago to
wish to challenge him, until it is too late.

What did Shakespeare gain if, as, I think, he followed the
hint in Cinthio? First, he heightened suspense: Iago's plot
hangs by a thread once Emilia's suspicions are aroused, even
if he manages to bluff it out in 4.2. Second, he reinforced 'the
human will to see things as they are not'. . . . Emilia, already
disillusioned with her husband, prefers not to ask too many
questions, fearing to discover things as they really are.

                  what he will do with it
Heaven knows, not I,
I nothing, but to please his fantasy.
                                                (3.3.301-33)

Emilia repays some attention: her developing relationship
with her husband and her developing moral involvement il-
lustrate Shakespeare's remarkable control of detail, which
in turn justifies those critics who think it their duty to peer
into the recesses of character and motive.

Bruised Brabantio, Sensitive Cassio, and Pitiful Roderigo

Harley Granville-Barker

Harley Granville-Barker (1877–1946) was a world-renowned stage actor, theatrical producer, and literary critic as well as a respected Shakespearean scholar. In this excerpt from the second volume of his famous *Prefaces to Shakespeare*, he briefly but insightfully analyzes the play's three minor but still crucial male characters: Brabantio (Desdemona's aggrieved father), Cassio (Othello's loyal officer whom Iago falsely implicates in a love affair with Desdemona), and Roderigo (one of Desdemona's former suitors, who becomes Iago's unwitting dupe).

Brabantio is redeemed from the convention of the hoodwinked father by a few specific strokes. He swings between extremes, from his high regard for Othello to insensate abuse of him, through a chill pardon for Desdemona, in which past tenderness still echoes, to the cutting farewell:

> She has deceived her father, and may thee.

He seems exceptionally credulous about

> spells and medicines bought of mountebanks . . .

but he takes a detached view of his own nature, "glad at soul" that he has no other child, since Desdemona's escape would teach him "tyranny, to hang clogs on them." He passes from a frantic bustle of pursuit:

> Raise all my kindred. . . .
> Call up my brother. . . .
> Some one way, some another. . . .
> At every house I'll call. . . .

to quiet, solitary dignity before the Senate, as from clamor for vengeance on Othello to the magnanimous

> If she confess that she was half the wooer,
> Destruction on my head, if my bad blame. . . .
> Light on the man!

And then and there, despite grief and defeat, he is capable of capping the Duke's encouraging platitudes with some very smooth irony. But it looks as if the shock and the strain may have broken him, and when he speaks of his "bruised heart" he means it. And later we hear that Desdemona's loss

> was mortal to him, and pure grief
> Shore his old thread in twain.

Cassio

The [1623 First] Folio's list of characters calls Cassio *an Honourable Lieutenant.* He is seemingly a man of gentle birth, and of education; Iago mocking at his "bookish theoric." He is the unwitting implement of evil, its stalking-horse, and his place in the play's scheme is that of an average, unheroic, well-meaning man caught between tragic extremes—of wickedness and of the nobility it betrays. His faults are failings, redeemable by his own recognition of them. But here he sways, haplessly, somewhat ridiculously, between extremes within himself. He knows that he has "very poor and unhappy brains for drinking," yet he yields from good nature to the claims of good fellowship, though he says, even as he does so, "it dislikes me." He is sensitive even to self-consciousness, and, beyond that, to the point of self-display. Having listened in disciplined silence to Othello's sentence on him, in his heart-felt outburst to Iago, the

> Reputation, reputation, reputation. O, I have lost my reputation! I have lost the immortal part of myself, and what remains is bestial. My reputation, Iago, my reputation!

we remark that he is listening, not unappreciatively, to the sounds of his own despair. Such misery does not strike deep, nor last long; its enjoyment is soon exhausted. Iago tactfully gives it scope, and Cassio, disburdened, not only accepts his optimistic advice without question, but will "betimes in the morning . . . beseech the virtuous Desdemona" to plead his cause. For may not Othello's anger dissolve as easily—so this mood bids him hope—as has the bitterness of his own remorse? The man is mercurial [changeable in temperament]. He is a lightweight. But there is with that something boyish about him, and appealing. Despite his despair, he thinks to bring musicians to play the customary nuptial *aubade* beneath Othello's windows; an ingenuous piece of propitiation. He is a romantic soul. We have him, during those first moments in Cyprus, rhapsodizing over "the divine Desdemona." He is gaily gallant, finds it good fun to claim a kiss of welcome from Emilia. And Iago's "profane and liberal wit" having served its purpose while they all wait anxiously for news of Othello, he takes his turn at distracting Desdemona, more delicately and intimately, yet openly and respectfully, galling Iago with envy of his address in "such tricks," in kissing his "three fingers" and playing "the sir," having already—how thoughtlessly—patronizingly disparaged his Ancient's good breeding to her, with that

> He speaks home, madam: you may relish him more in the soldier than in the scholar.

But he has a finer sense than all this shows of Desdemona's quality. She is for him—the epithet springs spontaneously—"the virtuous Desdemona." Nor will he join in the accepted marriage pleasantries, meets Iago's ribald

> Our general . . . hath not yet made wanton the night with her, and she is sport for Jove.

with a cold snub. And her "bounteous" compassion on him when he is in trouble raises respect to very reverence.

PUPPETS IN IAGO'S HANDS

His attitude towards Bianca is of a piece with the rest of him. She is his mistress, she is "a customer," and he scoffs merrily at "the monkey's" pretense that he means to marry her. But he treats her, even as Shakespeare does, decently and humanely. He does not care to have her pursue him in the street—who would?—and, being what she is, she must put up with a blunt

> leave me for this time. . . .
> I do attend here on the general
> And think it no addition, nor my wish
> To have him see me womaned.

nor does he scruple to round on her pretty sharply when she vexes him. But, this apart, she is his "most fair Bianca," his "sweet love." He excuses himself with courteous insincerity for a week's neglect of her, protesting that he loves her, paying her in that coin too. He is a gentleman, and she, as the phrase goes, is no better than she should be. But he would never be guilty, to her face or behind her back, of the grossness of Iago's "This is the fruits of whoring."

The weakness which lets him drink when he knows he cannot carry his liquor is matched by his broken resolve to break with Bianca. He has kept it for a week; and, confiding to Iago what an infatuated nuisance she is, he protests:

> Well. I must leave her company.

Yet a moment later, after she has told him in a fit of tantrums to come and sup with her that same night or see her no more, Iago dryly demanding if he means to, he answers shruggingly:

> Faith, I intend so.

the full truth being, it would seem, that he is both secretly flattered by her scandalous infatuation for him—he makes the most of it:

> She falls me thus about my neck. . . . So hangs and lolls and weeps upon me; so hales and pulls me. . . .

—and not a little afraid of her. It is at this point in the play that he, with Othello, is brought to the lowest pitch of indignity; puppets the two of them in Iago's hands, the one turned eavesdropper, the other fatuously vaunting his conquest of a light-o'-love.

But a worthier finish is reserved him. For his would-be murder he utters no harsher reproach than

> Dear general, I never gave you cause.

and his epitaph upon Othello is fitly felt:

> For he was great of heart.

And—though here, if the story were to have a sequel, we might question Senatorial judgment—he is left to rule in Cyprus.

RODERIGO

The Folio is as exact with its "Roderigo, *a gull'd Gentleman*"; but to this stock figure also Shakespeare gives human substance. It tells another tale of moral degradation; Iago the unresisted instrument. For Roderigo begins as an honorable suitor for Desdemona's hand; and, for his service in sounding the alarm, he converts Brabantio straightway from the

> In honest plainness thou hast heard me say
> My daughter is not for thee. . . .

to a

> good Roderigo, I'll deserve your pains.

And what could be more correct than the long, elaborate, pedantically parenthetical address to the newly wakened and distracted father at the window, with which he justifies his interference?

> I beseech you,
> If't be your pleasure and most wise consent,
> As partly I find it is . . .

—a mild effort at sarcasm—

> that your fair daughter,
> At this odd-even and dull watch of the night,
> Transported with no worse nor better guard
> But with a knave of common hire, a gondolier . . .

—as who might say today: carried off in a taxi-cab, not even a private car!—

> To the gross clasps of a lascivious Moor—
> If this be known to you, and your allowance . . .

—sarcasm again!—

> We then have done you bold and saucy wrongs;
> But if you know not this, my manners tell me
> We have your wrong rebuke . . .

—a neat antithesis!—

> Do not believe,
> That, from the sense of all civility,
> I thus would play the trifle with your reverence:
> Your daughter, if you have not given her leave . . .

—he fancies his sarcasm—

> I say again, hath made a gross revolt,
> Tying her duty, beauty, wit and fortunes,
> In an extravagant and wheeling stranger . . .

—his vocabulary too!—

> Of here and everywhere. . . .

—and could listen to his own eloquence all night. We see Iago in the background, a-grin at the foolish exhibition.

Roderigo's renewed hopes soar high, then, as he sticks by the grateful Brabantio and follows him to the Senate, but only to collapse again utterly upon the surrendering of Desdemona to Othello. He stands there mute, would be left alone and ignored even by Iago, did he not at last utter a plaintive

> What will I do, thinkest thou? . . .
> I will incontinently drown myself.

—the "silly gentleman" at his silliest, most pitiable, least unlikable.

A MUDDLED MIND, A PITIFUL FOOL

He goes to the devil with his eyes open, yet blindly. His poor mind is no better than a sounding board for Iago's sophistries [plausible sounding but false arguments]. Yet he takes each step downward most advisedly, and even in admitting his folly he persists in it. He is an incorrigible fool. To put money—for Iago—in his purse, to follow the wars—and Desdemona—he will sell all his land, uproot and leave himself to the mercy of events. And his moral sense is as feeble and obscure as his mind is muddled. Since he cannot win Desdemona for his wife, he may get her—Iago persuades him—as a mistress, may cuckold Othello. There will be manly satisfaction in that. But when he hears that she is in love with Cassio:

> Why, 'tis not possible. . . . I cannot believe that in her; she's full of most blessed condition.

And it is not, seemingly, that he thinks his own charms, given their chance, would make way with her, for he listens, unprotesting, to their most unflattering comparison with Cassio's. A less convinced, a more unconvincing, libertine there could hardly be. Finally, however, patience and cash exhausted, he protests, and, in a prepared oration, following the one he launched at Brabantio's window, he calls Iago to account. He has been let in—such is the tone of it—for a pretty poor investment, financially and morally too, and must now save what he can from the wreck:

> The jewels you have had from me to deliver to Desdemona would half have corrupted a votarist: you have told me she hath received them and returned me expectations and comforts of sudden respect and acquaintance; but I find none. . . . I will make myself known to Desdemona. If she will return me my jewels, I will give over my suit and repent my unlawful solicitation; if not, assure yourself I will seek satisfaction of you.

Is there, after all, any real vice in the creature? He sees himself handed back his jewels while he makes Desdemona yet another carefully prepared little speech of polite regret for ever having dreamed of committing adultery with her. And his amorous advances, we may suspect, would have been hardly more formidable.

But if there is no passion in him, evil or good, to stimulate, such little mind as he possesses Iago does most successfully corrupt. The denigration of Desdemona is left to sink in; the less he believes in her virtue, the readier he will be to continue his pursuit of her; his final complaint is that the jewels have had no effect. The "satisfying reasons" he has received for Cassio's death we do not hear; but an echo of them can be caught in the callous

> 'Tis but a man gone.

with which, craven in his ambush, he draws a clumsy sword. With Iago for guide, he has traveled from the lovelorn folly of

> I will incontinently drown myself.

to this. Even so, he is no more of a success as a murderer than he has been as an adulterer; and his bravo's

> Villain, thou diest!

is promptly changed, with Cassio's sword between his own ribs instead, into an abjectly repentant

> O, villain that I am!

A last disillusion is due; his mentor's face mockingly grinning, his friend's dagger stuck in him—

> O damned Iago; O inhuman dog!

Disillusion indeed! But he is so futile a fool that we spare him some pity.

CHAPTER 3

Central Themes and Ideas Developed in *Othello*

Many-Faceted Jealousy Leads to Tragedy

Lily B. Campbell

In this excerpt from her book *Shakespeare's Tragic Heroes*, noted Shakespearean scholar Lily B. Campbell explains why she, like a majority of other scholars, views *Othello* as "a tragedy of jealousy." She first explains how Renaissance scholars viewed the passion of jealousy, citing some of their works. Jealousy was then seen as many-faceted, incorporating elements of hatred, envy, possessiveness, and revenge; Campbell shows, act by act, how Shakespeare skillfully developed these individual passions, never losing sight of their integral role in the overriding, and in this case ultimately fatal, passion of jealousy.

Othello has suffered less in its modern interpretation than any other of Shakespeare's tragedies, it would seem. So insistently did Shakespeare keep this tragedy unified about the theme of jealousy and the central victims of the passion, so obviously did he mould his plot about the black Moor and the cunning Iago and the victims of their jealousy that no interpreter has been able to ignore the obvious intention of the author. Yet if we study the contemporary interpretations of the passion here portrayed, we find that Shakespeare was following in detail a broader and more significant analysis of the passion than has in modern days been understood. The play is, however, clearly a study in jealousy and in jealousy as it affects those of different races.

DEFINING JEALOUSY

Jealousy was, in the thinking of the Renaissance, not one of the simple or elementary passions but a derivative or compounded passion. It is a species of envy, which is in turn a species of hatred. Hatred finds its opposite in love and is op-

Excerpted from Lily B. Campbell, *Shakespeare's Tragic Heroes: Slaves of Passion.* Copyright Cambridge University Press 1930. Reprinted by permission of Cambridge University Press.

posed to love. Envy is opposed to mercy. Yet while jealousy is opposed to love, it rises often from love. And like envy it has something of the grief or fear that comes from seeing another in possession of that which we would possess solely for ourselves, or from fearing that another may possess it. It is this curious mingling of love and hatred with grief or fear that we see in jealousy. . . .

Though jealousy is thus compounded, it still partakes of the nature of hatred. And hatred brings in its wake anger and revenge. . . .

So likewise do envy and jealousy bring anger and a desire for revenge.

But since jealousy is also a species of envy, we need to examine the nature of envy. And of envy there are four kinds . . . (1) the envy that we feel because the profit of others is so great as to hurt our own; (2) the envy that we feel because the welfare or profit of another has not happened to us (being in reality a kind of covetousness); (3) the envy which makes us unwilling any other should have a good which we desire, or which we have wished for and could not get; and (4) the envy which makes us feel ourselves hurt when others receive any good.

The most complete study of jealousy during the Renaissance was made in an Italian work by [the sixteenth-century scholar Benedetto] Varchi, which was translated into English and published with notes by Robert Tofte in 1615 as *The Blazon of Jealousie.* . . . Here again the fact that jealousy is a kind of envy is emphasized. That the kinds of jealousy are related to the kinds of envy is at once apparent from Varchi's analysis, for he classifies the kinds of jealousy:

> (1) Eyther when wee would not have that any one should obtayne, that which wee our selves have already gotten: (2) Or that which wee wish and desire to obtayne: (3) Or which wee have laboured and endevoured, following it in chase, and yet could never gayne the same.

According to this author, jealousy comes by reason (1) of pleasure, (2) of passion, (3) of property or right, and (4) of honour. And he defines these terms in the passages which I quote:

> Jealousie commeth of Pleasure, when wee estimate and prise the delight wee take in the Partie we love, at so high a rate, as we would engrosse it wholy unto our selves, and when wee thinke, or imagine, it will decrease and waxe lesse, if it should be communicated, or lent unto another:

Jealousie proceedeth from Passion, when we covet to enjoy or possesse that which we most love and like, wonderfully fearing lest we should loose the possession thereof, as if our Mistresse should become a secret sweet Friend unto another man:

Thirdly, *Jealousie* springeth from the Propertie or Right that wee have, when we (enjoying our Lady or Mistresse) would have her soly and wholy unto our selves; without being able (by any meanes) to suffer or endure, that another man should have any part or interest in her, any way, or at any time:

Lastly, *Jealousie* commeth in respect of a mans Reputation and Honour, according as his nature is, or as his Breeding hath beene, or after the fashion and manner of the Country, in which hee is borne and liveth, because (in this point) divers are the opinions of men, and as contrary are the Customes of Countries, whereupon they say, that the Southerne Nations, and such as dwell in hot Regions are very Jealous; eyther because they are much given and enclined unto Love naturally: or else for that they hold it a great disparagement and scandall, to have their Wifes, or their Mistresses taynted with the foule blot of Unchastitie: which thing those that are of contrary Regions, and such as live under the North-Pole, take not so deepe at the heart. . . .

It is easily seen, then, why Shakespeare chose a story which could centre the study of jealousy about those of different races, and why Othello's great defence of his own actions at the last is significant:

For nought I did in hate, but all in honour.

Just as the grief-oppressed Hamlet was the inevitable choice for the subject of a play in which revenge was motivated by a ghost . . . so Othello is the perfect choice for a study of the passion of jealousy, since in him we can see the working of the passion in one of a race to whom it is natural to be jealous. . . .

PERFECT HATRED IN HIS HEART

It is in order, then, to see what Shakespeare has to say about Othello at the opening of the play. From the first we hear the fact insistently repeated that he is a Moor, that he has thick lips, that Desdemona has chosen to go to his sooty bosom. Yet we are told that he is of noble birth, that war and adventure have been his nurses, that he may be considered a barbarian and yet that the Venetian state has found him so valuable in action that he cannot be expelled, no matter what offence may be found in him. His vaunting has won him his wife; his actions have won him the confidence of the state. His noble nature is not questioned even by Iago.

Iago, it would seem, is of the melancholy humour, fitly chosen for the villain in a tragedy of jealousy. . . .

But Iago is, as we might expect, not merely jealous. With him jealousy is but one phase of envy, and in his heart is perfect hatred. In him passion has already worked its destruction. . . .

It is then on a theme of hate that the play opens. It is a hate of inveterate anger. It is a hate that is bound up with envy. Othello has preferred to be his lieutenant a military theorist, one Michael Cassio, over the experienced soldier Iago, to whom has fallen instead the post of "his Moorship's ancient". Roderigo questions Iago:

> Thou told'st me thou didst hold him in thy hate.

And the reply is a torrent of proof of the hatred for Othello that has almost exceeded the envy of Cassio because he possesses the prize which Iago has sought to obtain for himself. . . .

Just as Iago is envious because Cassio possesses the prize which he had sought to get for himself, and as he hates Othello as the one who preferred Cassio to himself, so Roderigo is presented as one who is the victim of jealousy because Othello has got possession of the girl whom he has followed and could not gain. So much is apparent from Brabantio's hostile greeting to his first warning of Desdemona's departure:

> I have charg'd thee not to haunt about my doors.
> In honest plainness thou hast heard me say
> My daughter is not for thee; . . .

And as the reluctant Brabantio is finally roused to take heed of the warning given by these two envious and jealous alarmers, we hear Iago reaffirm the nature of his envy and his hate as he decides it will not be well for him to be recognized as an agent in giving the alarm against the Moor:

> Though I do hate him as I do hell-pains,
> Yet, for necessity of present life,
> I must show out a flag and sign of love,
> Which is indeed but sign. . . .

HATE BALANCED BY LOVE

Then in the midst of the commotion brewed in the night by the news of war and the news of Othello's marriage, we find that, having begun the play on the note of hate and envy, Shakespeare is now balancing love and hate, and the whole of the first act is seen to be as well an anatomy of love as of hate. . . .

The simple and noble love of Othello and Desdemona is known to us all, but it must be noted that Desdemona . . . loves both her father and her husband in reason. She says to her father:

> My noble father,
> I do perceive here a divided duty.
> To you I am bound for life and education;
> My life and education both do learn me
> How to respect you; you are the lord of duty;
> I am hitherto your daughter. But here's my husband;
> And so much duty as my mother show'd
> To you, preferring you before her father,
> So much I challenge that I may profess
> Due to the Moor, my lord.

That her love is that perfect love which philosophers found to blend the love of body and of mind is evident also in the familiar:

> That I did love the Moor to live with him,
> My downright violence and storm of fortunes
> May trumpet to the world. My heart's subdu'd
> Even to the very quality of my lord.
> I saw Othello's visage in his mind,
> And to his honours and his valiant parts.
> Did I my soul and fortunes consecrate.

And she begs to be allowed to go with him as he goes to war.

That Othello's love too is a love that is noble and perfect is evident in his simple:

> She lov'd me for the dangers I had pass'd,
> And I lov'd her that she did pity them. . . .

Against this tempered and noble love is pictured the love of Roderigo. His love is intemperate, he is over-fond, he wishes to commit self-murder rather than to live in such torment, he is ashamed and yet cannot find virtue to overcome that of which he is ashamed. Above all, he will secure his love by foul means and shamefully. His passion controls his will even though his judgment acts in opposition to it.

To him Iago explains his philosophy of love, and because he explains also with absolute explicitness the Shakespearean villain, his words are of great import. To Iago love is merely "a lust of the blood and a permission of the will". Self-love, which is in the thinking of Shakespeare's day the mother of all vices, is the only love that Iago respects. To Roderigo's talk of virtue he exclaims:

> Virtue! a fig! 't is in ourselves that we are thus or thus. Our
> bodies are our gardens, to the which our wills are gardeners;

so that if we will plant nettles, or sow lettuce, set hyssop and weed up thyme, supply it with one gender of herbs, or distract it with many, either to have it sterile with idleness, or manured with industry, why, the power and corrigible authority of this lies in our wills. If the balance of our lives had not one scale of reason to poise another of sensuality, the blood and baseness of our natures would conduct us to most preposterous conclusions; but we have reason to cool our raging motions, our carnal stings, our unbitted lusts, whereof I take this that you call love to be a sect or scion.

It is thus that the villain is defined. Will is directed to the gaining of ends set by passion and judged by reason. The passion which escapes reason and leads men on to their destruction is the passion which marks the tragic hero. But the passion which sets the ends and has the means judged by reason is the passion which we have already seen is mortal sin. And such is the passion that has brought the judgment and the will into its service in Iago, and in the other villains. In Roderigo even there is still a fight between passion and reason; in Iago there is no fight, for the higher is made to serve the lower. . . .

HATRED DEMANDS REVENGE

The second act of *Othello* opens with the peace after war, the calm after the storm, perfect happiness after the evils that make happiness more prized. Othello is moved to exclaim:

> If it were now to die,
> 'T were now to be most happy; for, I fear,
> My soul hath her content so absolute
> That not another comfort like to this
> Succeeds in unknown fate. . . .

But peace and calm and love are all to be broken by the villainy which will lead its victims one by one to passion and thence to self-destruction. Iago reveals his machiavellianism insistently. First we see him watching Cassio's greeting of Desdemona and concluding:

> With as little a web as this will I ensnare as great a fly as Cassio.

Then we see him working upon Roderigo, urging that Desdemona loved the Moor but for his "fantastical lies", that she loved him too violently:

> When the blood is made dull with the act of sport, there should be, again to inflame it, and to give satiety a fresh appetite, loveliness in favour, sympathy in years, manners, and beauties; all which the Moor is defective in. . . .

The hatred which he feels toward Othello demands revenge; and revenge demands not only a wife for a wife; it demands also that Othello shall feel this same gnawing jealousy which is destroying him. He will use Cassio to this purpose, but no sooner does he turn his thoughts to Cassio than he suspects him too and feeds his jealousy with thinking. The rest of the play is taken up largely with the execution of his plan, for he does indeed put the Moor "into a jealousy so strong That judgement cannot cure" and swiftly we see him practising upon Othello's "peace and quiet Even to madness". . . .

Thus Iago, by skilfully rousing each victim to passion, prepares for his final plot which shall touch even Desdemona and "turn her virtue into pitch" to Othello's jaundiced sight. . . .

THE KEYNOTE OF OTHELLO'S JEALOUSY

Act III is the record of the success of the plots so devised. Cassio entreats Desdemona and is seen by Iago and Othello. Her entreaties to Othello win him to her opinion, it would seem, and he cries prophetically:

> Excellent wretch! Perdition catch my soul,
> But I do love thee! and when I love thee not,
> Chaos is come again.

Then as Iago commences his subtle suggestion of evil, as he confesses that his jealousy often "shapes faults that are not", we find that he begins his attack on Othello to rouse his jealousy by talking about his good name. In other words, the fourth cause of jealousy as given in *The Blazon of Jealousie*, is appropriately chosen here to stir up passion in this man of the black complexion. In the passage from this work quoted earlier in the chapter, it was said:

> Jealousie commeth in respect of a mans Reputation and Honor, according as his nature is, or as his Breeding hath beene, or after the fashion and manner of the Country, in which hee is borne and liveth. . . .

Tofte's note on this passage of Varchi said:

> Honor, is the Reputation and Credit, or the good name and Fame, of a Man, which the generous Spirit priseth, at so high a rate, as before hee will have the same eclipst, hee will loose all his wealth, yea, and his dearest life. . . .

It is at once perceived that the note struck by Cassio in the second act in his "Reputation, reputation, reputation!"

speech is the same one that is now more significantly echoed by Iago:

> Good name in man and woman, dear my lord,
> Is the immediate jewel of their souls.
> Who steals my purse steals trash; 't is something, nothing;
> 'T was mine, 't is his, and has been slave to thousands;
> But he that filches from me my good name
> Robs me of that which not enriches him,
> And makes me poor indeed.

This is the keynote of Othello's jealousy, as it should be the keynote of the jealousy of the alien black man who was general in the army of Venice. And Shakespeare characteristically harps the note, in Cassio, in Iago, in Othello. . . .

THE SLAVE OF PASSION

As Othello is left alone, the workings of the monster in his heart are apparent. It is now the jealousy that through pleasure and passion felt in and for the loved one advances to jealousy that is the jealousy of property. . . .

Thus we hear Othello:

> I am abus'd; and my relief
> Must be to loathe her. O curse of marriage,
> That we can call these delicate creatures ours,
> And not their appetites! I had rather be a toad
> And live upon the vapour of a dungeon,
> Then keep a corner of the thing I love
> For others' uses.

Now indeed Othello is become the man who is described by Varchi:

> for this strange Maladie engendreth a continuall and a perpetuall discontentment and disquietnesse in the minde, for that hee is not able, nor hath any power to give over from vexing himselfe. . . .

Othello himself cries:

> thou hast set me on the rack.
> I swear 't is better to be much abus'd
> Than but to know a little.

And then we find him torturing himself with the thoughts of Cassio's kisses on Desdemona's lips, and he reiterates the property idea in his talk of being robbed.

From this time on, Othello has become the slave of passion. As he cries farewell to the tranquil mind, to content, to war and his occupation, as he demands that Iago prove his love a whore, as he threatens Iago and begs for proof at the same time, he is finally led almost to the verge of madness in his return to a discussion of honour, Desdemona's honour this time:

> Her name, that was as fresh
> As Dian's visage, is now begrim'd and black
> As mine own face. If there be cords, or knives,
> Poison, or fire, or suffocating streams,
> I'll not endure it. Would I were satisfied!

Iago says truly:

> I see, sir, you are eaten up with passion;

and it is well to recall that Othello's speech when he came to quiet the brawl of Cassio marked the beginning of his giving way to passion which is climaxed here.

From this time Othello lives in a world which has become chaos through his own passion. Now jealousy is seen in its close kinship with that anger which demands revenge. To Iago's tale of Cassio's dream, he exclaims only:

> I'll tear her all to pieces. . . .

OTHELLO DEMANDS PUNISHMENT

Now that Othello is roused by jealousy to anger and to a hungry desire for revenge, it is of anger that is opposed to love and of the impatient desire for revenge that we hear. His speeches are full of threats: "How shall I murder him, Iago", and "I would have him nine years a-killing". But as his thoughts turn to Desdemona, even as he decides that "she shall not live", grief overwhelms him, and he commences to rehearse her claims to being loved, and to lament "the pity of it".

But to Iago's suggestion that if her offence does not injure Othello, it injures no one, Othello cries:

> I will chop her into messes. Cuckold me!

His mind is again centred on his own injury. . . .

The revenge of Iago has demanded that Cassio be punished and that Othello be made to feel the same madness of jealousy that he has felt. The revenge of Othello demands now that both Cassio and Desdemona die for having caused him grief, for daring to injure his honour, for having cuckolded him. He demands poison, but Iago is more just in his revenges:

> Do it not with poison; strangle her in her bed, even the bed she hath contaminated.

And Othello replies:

> Good, good; the justice of it pleases; very good.

Thus revenge always cries for justice and for that cunning justice that fits punishment to offence.

As Lodovico arrives to summon Othello to Venice and to bring word that the government of Cyprus shall be placed in Cassio's care, the angry Othello has advanced so far in anger and rage that he strikes Desdemona, mocks her grief as "well-painted passion", and welcomes Lodovico, with such insane jibes that the astonished man can but question Iago:

> Is this the noble Moor whom our full Senate
> Call all in all sufficient? Is this the nature
> Whom passion could not shake? whose solid virtue
> The shot of accident nor dart of chance
> Could neither graze nor pierce?

And then to Iago's wise grief he adds:

> Are his wits safe? Is he not light of brain?. . .

THE INNOCENT SUFFER WITH THE GUILTY

The last act but spreads before us the devastation wrought by passion. Roderigo is fatally wounded in the fray which comes as the result of his attempt to kill Cassio. The Moor goes to his task of killing his wife in the name of justice:

> Thy bed, lust-stain'd, shall with lust's blood be spotted.

And in the second scene, the scene of the murder, he cries again as he looks upon the sleeping Desdemona and kisses her:

> Oh, balmy breath, thou dost almost persuade
> Justice to break her sword!

It is this insistence upon the passion which makes men try to take the place of God, and by private revenge execute the laws of God that makes *Othello* significant in the tragedy of its time. Othello sees his acts as the expression of justice, worked out in the most perfect balance of deed and punishment. And yet Shakespeare shows us the passion which impels him to revenge rather than the judgment which alone can mete out justice. Desdemona makes us see him indeed as passion's slave and not as the executioner of God's justice when she cries:

> Alas, why gnaw you so your nether lip?
> Some bloody passion shakes your very frame. . . .

The end of the play in its uncovering of villainy and its terrific exhibiting of grief and repentance need not be rehearsed in detail. But Othello's final defence must be carefully considered:

> An honourable murderer, if you will;
> For nought I did in hate, but all in honour.

And at the last:

> Then must you speak
> Of one that lov'd not wisely but too well;
> Of one not easily jealous, but being wrought
> Perplex'd in the extreme; of one whose hand,
> Like the base Indian, threw a pearl away
> Richer than all his tribe.

It must be remembered, however, that Othello executes the same justice upon himself that he had tried to execute upon Desdemona, that he kills himself and falls upon the murderous bed with the cry:

> I kiss'd thee ere I kill'd thee: no way but this,
> Killing myself, to die upon a kiss.

And Cassio pays him his final tribute, "For he was great of heart".

At the close of the play Brabantio is dead of his grief over the marriage of his daughter; Roderigo is dead through the retribution that has come upon him in his attempt to gain the means to his unholy love; Emilia is dead through the angry vengeance of her husband; Desdemona has been murdered in Othello's attempt to revenge his own jealous honour; Othello has killed himself in his final grief; Iago awaits his punishment. But most truly has the play pictured the fact that

> Now as there is no wicked affection, which carrieth not about, it owne torment to take vengeance thereof by the just judgement of God, so this of envy passeth all the rest in this respect.

And we see the significance of Othello's last words to Iago:

> I'd have thee live;
> For, in my sense, 't is happiness to die.

Again Shakespeare has pictured a passion in all its associations. Here jealousy, which is compounded of the hatred which is envy and of grief that must be associated with envy, is pictured in all of its phases. The variants of love are shown; the variants of envy are likewise depicted. Again the passion studied is shown in different people of different races. . . .

And again passion has wrought its deadly work: drink has ministered to passion and caused disaster; passion has resulted in epilepsy and then in fury and rage and finally in murder. And passion has again caused the innocent to suffer with the guilty.

Cold Reason Overcomes the Power of Love

Robert B. Heilman

The theme of love runs, in various forms, throughout
Othello, not only in the obvious, overt love Othello feels
for Desdemona, and she for him, but also in the way
Iago reacts to their love (as well as love in general), with
envy and hatred. In this essay, literary scholar Robert B.
Heilman contends that Iago has an inability to believe
in, take seriously, or understand the concept of romantic love, "the magic bringer of harmony between those
who are wildly different." To Iago, such love is akin to
witchcraft, another force or realm that he cannot
fathom or in any way control. (Thus, says Heilman,
Shakespeare uses the concept of witchcraft as a metaphor for love.) In this view, Iago ultimately uses cold
reason (wit) to overcome the power of mysterious love.

Theme is ideational raw material, open to all playwrights or to
one playwright repeatedly; thematic form results from the
molding of the raw material that takes place in a single com-
positional experience; it is a unique shaping of the action as this
is seen in terms of the ideational substance. "Love" appears in
diverse dramatic structures in *Romeo*, *Antony*, and *Othello*. Our
business here is to see how it is "structured" in *Othello*.

REASON MAY SERVE THE IRRATIONAL

Before coming directly to the forming of the love-theme that dif-
ferentiates *Othello* from the other Shakespeare plays that utilize
the same theme, I turn arbitrarily to Iago to inspect a distin-
guishing mark of his of which the relevance to thematic form in
the play will appear a little later. When Iago with unperceived
scoffing reminds Roderigo, who is drawn with merciless attraction to the unreachable Desdemona, that love effects an un-

Excerpted from Robert B. Heilman, "Wit and Witchcraft: Thematic Form in *Othello*,"
Arizona Quarterly 12 (1956). Reprinted by permission of the Regents of the University
of Arizona.

wonted nobility in men, he states a doctrine which he "knows" is true but in which he may not "believe." Ennoblement by love is a real possibility in men, but Iago has to view it with bitterness and to try to undermine it. With his spontaneous antipathy to spiritual achievement, he must in principle deny the mysterious transformation of personality; instinctively he is the observer of all these habits that suggest infinite corruptibility as the comprehensive human truth. He is the believer in shrewd observation and in corruption in whose credo, which is not altogether unique, man is a union of lusting, folly, and plotting.

Good sense, hard sense, common sense, no nonsense, rationality—all these terms, we may suppose, are ones which Iago might consider as defining his perspective. As he plays against Othello with his game of honest and loving friend, he uses words that put him on that side of the fence. First he can't tell Othello his "thoughts" (about Cassio) because of his "manhood, honesty, or *wisdom*" (3.3.153–54); a little later he finds "*reason*" to tell them (193). Othello considers him "*wise*" (4.1.75). While privately Iago may deny his love and kid his honesty, he takes his brains seriously. "Thus do I ever make my *fool* my purse," he boasts; to spend time with Roderigo otherwise, "Mine own gain'd *knowledge* should profane" (1.3.389–90). Othello is to be treated like an *ass* (1.3.408; 2.1.318). Iago applies the term *fool* successively to Roderigo (2.3.53), Cassio (2.3.359), Desdemona (4.1.186), and Emilia (4.2.148) and condescends to fools "credulous" and "gross" (3.3.404; 4.1.46). His view of himself as the clearheaded manipulator of gulls is significantly unchallenged despite the barrage of derogatory rhetoric eventually aimed at him. He remains the "smart man," apt in "deals," scornful of "suckers.". . .

Making a fool of someone else is an aesthetic demonstration of intellectual superiority. It is implicitly partial, temporary; a comic episode after which life goes on. Let this exploit in self-aggrandizement expand with the full pressure of passion, and that attack becomes an ultimate one against sanity: Iago's design to put Othello "into a jealousy so strong/That judgment cannot cure," driving him "even to madness" (2.1.310–11, 320). It is the extreme revenge possible to the man of "reason," a chaos that logically extends and completes the other modes of chaos which Iago instinctively seeks, in a variety of ways, at all stages of the action. Twice again he speaks of Othello's madness as a likelihood or as a formal objective (4.1.56, 101), and his program works well enough to make Lodovico inquire about Othello's mental soundness (4.1.280) and to make Othello express a doubt about his own sanity (5.2.111). Madness spreads: Emilia fears lest Desdemona "run mad" (3.3.317), Othello cries to her that he is "glad to see you mad" (4.1.250), and she in turn fears his "fury" (4.1.32). But the planned madness eventually recoils upon its creator: "What, are you mad?" is Iago's response when Emilia tells the truth about what he has done (5.2.194).

Such points in the auxiliary theme of madness (a slender anticipation of what will be done in *Lear*) mark the course of rational Iago. Insofar as he identifies rationality and wisdom with his own purpose, he is close enough to Everyman; but he is sharply individualized, and at the same time made

---

IAGO ASSOCIATES LOVE WITH WITCHCRAFT

In this speech, from the long scene in which Iago convinces Othello of Desdemona's infidelity, Iago skillfully and deceptively exploits the concept of love, at one point associating it with witchcraft.

IAGO. I am glad of this; for now I shall have reason
To show the love and duty that I bear you
With franker spirit. Therefore, as I am bound,
Receive it from me. I speak not yet of proof.
Look to your wife; observe her well with Cassio;
Wear your eyes thus: not jealous nor secure.
I would not have your free and noble nature
Out of self-bounty be abused. Look to't.
I know our country disposition well:
In Venice they do let heaven see the pranks
They dare not show their husbands; their best conscience
Is not to leave't undone, but kept unknown.

OTHELLO. Dost thou say so?

IAGO. She did deceive her father, marrying you;
And when she seemed to shake and fear your looks,
She loved them most.

OTHELLO.   And so she did.

IAGO.   Why, go to then!
She that so young could give out such a seeming
To seel her father's eyes up close as oak—
He thought 'twas witchcraft. But I am much to blame.
I humbly do beseech you of your pardon
For too much loving you.

Othello 3.3.193–214, ed. Alvin Kernan. New York: New American Library, 1963, p. 100.

the representative of a recognizable human class, when the drama reveals that his purposes require the irrationalizing of life for everyone else. Of the insights that create Iago, none is deeper than the recognition that a cool rationality may itself bring about or serve the irrational. . . .

WIT AND WITCHCRAFT

Reason as an ally of evil is a subject to which Shakespeare keeps returning, as if fascinated, but in different thematic forms as he explores different counter-forces. . . . Although Iago, as we saw, does not take seriously the ennobling power of love, he does not fail to let us know what he does take seriously. When, in his fake oath of loyalty to "wrong'd Othello," he vows "'The execution of his wit, hands, heart'" (3.3.466), Iago's words give a clue to the truth: his heart is his malice, his hands literally wound Cassio and kill Roderigo, and his wit is the genius that creates all the strategy. How it enters into the dialectic of structure, or the thematic form, is made clear in one of Iago's promises to Roderigo that he shall have Desdemona: "if sanctimony and a frail vow betwixt an erring barbarian and a supersubtle Venetian be not too hard for my wits and all the tribe of hell, thou shalt enjoy her" (1.3.362–66). "Tribe of hell" is somewhat rhetorical; the real antagonist is "my wits"—set against the rival power of love, which he cannot tolerate. But even beyond Iago's own conscious battle, his brains against a vow of love, there is a symbolic conflict in the heart of the drama. And for this symbolic conflict Iago . . . gives us a name by the words he chooses:

> Thou know'st we work by wit, and not by witchcraft;
> And wit depends on dilatory time.
>
> (2.2.378–79)

Wit and *witchcraft*: in this antithesis is the symbolic structure, or the thematic form, of *Othello*. By witchcraft, of course, Iago means conjuring and spells to induce desired actions and states of being. But as a whole the play dramatically develops another meaning of *witchcraft* and forces upon us an awareness of that meaning: *witchcraft* is a metaphor for love. The "magic in the web" of the handkerchief, as Othello calls it (3.4.69), extends into the fiber of the whole drama. Love is a magic bringer of harmony between those who are widely different (Othello and Desdemona), and it can be a magic transformer of personality; its ultimate power is fittingly marked by the miracle of Desdemona's voice speaking from beyond life, pronouncing forgiveness to the Othello who has murdered her (5.2.124–25). Such events lie outside the realm of "wit"—of the reason, cunning, and wisdom on which Iago rests—and this wit must be hostile to them. Wit must always strive to conquer witchcraft, and there is an obvious sense in which it should conquer, but there is another sense in which, though it try, it should not and cannot succeed; that, we may say, is what *Othello* is "about." Whatever disaster it causes, wit fails in the end: it cuts itself off in a demonic silence before death (Iago's "last words" are "I never will speak word"—5.2.304), while witchcraft—love—speaks after death (Desdemona's last farewell).

Between the poles of wit and witchcraft, all the major characters in the play find their orientation. Emilia looks at a good deal of life through the Iago wit, but yields to the love for Desdemona which transforms her into a sacrificial figure. Under the influence of the Iago wit, Cassio, acting through Desdemona's friendly love, tries to high-pressure Othello into a charity (a revocation of his dismissal) that could come only spontaneously. Roderigo falls under the witchcraft of love, but, instead of letting it take effect as it might, to bring him death or renunciation, chooses Iago's wit game and plays for what he cannot have. Emilia and Desdemona, dying, are not creatures of wit: what we have called witchcraft has led them to a transrational achievement in spirit.

THE PROGRAM OF WIT VERSUS THE MIRACLE OF LOVE

The conflict of Desdemona and Iago for Othello can be called the conflict of love and hate, or the conflict of two different potentialities in the soul where both reside. It may also be called the conflict of wit and witchcraft for Othello. Though Othello seems to be all the naivete of Everyman, and Iago to be all his calculatingness and slyness, Othello gives himself more to wit than witchcraft because he and Iago, though in different degrees, have much in common . . . an inadequate selfhood that crops up in self-pity and an eye for slights and injuries, an uncriticized instinct to soothe one's own feeling by punishing others (with an air of moral propriety), the need to possess in one's own terms or destroy, an incapacity for love that is the other side of self-love. All this is in another realm from that of witchcraft. When Othello decides to follow Iago and be "wise" and "cunning," he adopts a new code: he will "see" the facts, get the "evidence," "prove" his case against Desdemona, and execute "justice" upon her. This is the program of "wit." Now this is not only utterly inappropriate to the occasion on which, under Iago's tutelage, Othello elects to use it, nor is it simply one of several possible errors; rather he adopts an attitude or belief or style which is the direct antithesis of another mode of thought and feeling which is open to him. He makes that particular wrong choice which is the logical opposite of the right choice open to him. He essays to reason when reason is not relevant: he substitutes a disastrous wit for a saving witchcraft. . . . Othello, the prime beneficiary of witchcraft, might win all its gifts had he the faith that would open him to its action; but he is short on faith, is seduced by wit (the two actions are simply two faces of the same experience), and ruined. He knew the first miracle of love, the thing given without claim, but cut himself off from the greater miracle, the transformation of self into a giver. His final failure is that, though he comes to recognize that he has been witless, he is never capacious enough in spirit to know how fully he has failed or how much he has thrown away. He never sees the full Desdemona witchcraft. . . .

THE VILLAIN OF MELODRAMA

Wit is Iago's instrument to compensate for what he does not have. He perversely hates and yet lusts after what he does not have (Desdemona as a person, and as a symbol of love), and he undertakes to disparage it, minimize it, debunk it, and destroy it. Rule-or-ruin becomes rule-by-ruining. He must fashion the world after his own image: "And knowing what I am, I know what she shall be" (4.1.74). So it pleases him to trap (he repeatedly uses the language of hunting and trapping) those who are unlike himself, by proclaiming virtues which he does not possess ("honest Iago," the friend of all). . . . Noisiness and vulgarity of style become him, though as a skilled actor he can simulate the amiable, contained, and discreet adviser and consoler. His most far-reaching method is to seduce others philosophically—to woo them from assumptions in which their salvation might lie (faith in the spiritual quality of others), to baser assumptions that will destroy them (their freedom to act in the light of the accepted unregeneracy of all about them). Iago the moral agent is akin to Iago the philosopher: there is a common element in stealing purses, stealing good names, and stealing ideas needed for survival.

In sociological terms we might allegorize Iago as the criminal type, in political as the self-seeking divisive force or the patrioteer or the power-seeker who will pay any price ... in mythical as The Enemy—the universal destroyer of ultimate values. Before all these, he is simply a human being, the apparent friend and lover of everybody. We think of these diverse tentative formulations only because he is so variously and richly set before us as the final outcome when certain potentialities of Everyman are freed to develop fully. There is no single way into this extraordinary characterization. As the spiritual have-not, Iago is universal, that is, many things at once, and of many times at once. He is our contemporary, and the special instances of his temper and style—as distinct from the Iagoism to which all men are liable—will be clear to whoever is alert to Shakespeare's abundant formulations. Seen in a limited and stereotyped form, he is the villain of all melodrama. . . . He could be placed among the angry and violent. But his truer place is down among those who act in fraud and malice—the lowest category of sinner who on earth had least of spiritual substance and relied most on wit. . . .

By an extraordinary composition of character Shakespeare has made Iago, literally or symbolically, share in all these modes of evil. . . . But he has also dramatized the hidden springs of evil action, the urgency and passion and immediacy of it. He contemplates, too, the evildoer's "potency" and man's defenselessness: but these he interprets tragically by making them, not absolute, but partly dependent on the flaws or desire of the victims themselves. In the *Othello* world, Iago, seductive as he is, is not an inevitable teacher. Whoever would, could learn from Desdemona. He would have the choice of wit or witchcraft.

Othello's Loss of Fame and Reputation Leads to His Self-Destruction

David L. Jeffrey and Patrick Grant

The importance of fame and reputation to a state or military leader or hero and the disgrace of losing such rank and honors constitute a prominent theme in *Othello*. In this well-considered essay, literary scholars David L. Jeffrey and Patrick Grant use biblical and other references to define the two main kinds of fame—good and bad. They then cite numerous lines and speeches from the play in which characters either state the importance of reputation (for instance, Iago's "Good name in man and woman . . . is the immediate jewel of their souls"), or bemoan the loss of reputation (as in Othello's agonized "Othello's occupation's gone!"). In the end, say Jeffrey and Grant, the title character kills himself, at least in part, because he feels that his loss of reputation has destroyed his life.

Othello dies in Cyprus because he cannot endure the ill-esteem of his peers in Venice, and their denigration of his good name. Granted, he suffers to realize he has been made to murder his wife as Iago's dupe, but he does not stab himself in a blind frenzy of grief for this reason, rather as one realizing that his power and command are taken off (5.2.332) and his reputation destroyed. It is possible, pursuing this line of thought, to interpret the main action of the play as basically concerned with good and bad fame. For it is an initial faulty attitude to fame that tinctures [stains] Othello's love for his wife and provides the opportunity for Iago to initiate the plot that destroys his master.

We must distinguish between earthly fame and heavenly fame, a contrast based on Scripture. A distinction between earthly vanity and heavenly glory is often made, for instance

Excerpted from David L. Jeffrey and Patrick Grant, "Reputation in *Othello*," *Shakespeare Studies*, vol. 6 (1970). (Endnotes in the original have been omitted from this reprint.)

in Galatians 1:10: "For do I now persuade men or God? Or do
I seek to please men? For if I yet pleased men, I should not be
the servant of Christ." . . . In [the writings of the fourth-century
Christian thinker] Augustine, the classic definition of the two
loves, *caritas* and *cupiditas,* one based on "the enjoyment of
God for His own sake, and the enjoyment of one's self and
one's neighbour in subordination to God," the other aiming at
"enjoying one's self and one's neighbor, and other corporeal
things, without reference to God," is central to the contrast
which underlies the important discussion of fame in *De Civi-
tate Dei* [*the City of God*] (5, 12–20). There Augustine distin-
guishes true glory based on the "love of righteousness" and the
"love of God," from the false glory of the pagans based only on
renown among men and "desire of human praise."

Distinctions, therefore, between such concepts as charity
and the law, the New and Old Testaments, the glory of God and
glory of men, are of the essence of the contrast between fame
or reputation which is good (based on the referral of personal
glory to God) and fame which is bad (based on glorification of
the self). As late in the seventeenth century as [English poet
John] Milton's *Paradise Regained,* this is the import of Christ's
reply to Satan, where Job is described as famous "in Heaven,
on earth, less known; / Where glory is false glory, attributed /
To things not glorious, men not worthy of fame." . . .

HIS MILITARY REPUTATION

Othello's love is conditioned from the beginning by his attitude to fame, and this, essentially, is what proves fatal to
him. . . . Othello is confident even before he meets the senate that the many times he has risked his personal safety for
the welfare of the state will stand in his favour before his ac-
cusers. He assures Iago that reputation will protect him:

> Let him do his spite;
> My services, which I have done the signiory,
> Shall out-tongue his complaints; 'tis yet to know—
> Which, when I know that boasting is an honour,
> I shall promulgate—I fetch my life and being
> From men of royal siege, and my demerits
> May speak unbonneted to as proud a fortune
> As this that I have reach'd. (1.2.17–24)

Although this attitude must appear to approach a view of reputation that errs by relying too heavily on earthly fame, it is
nevertheless true that Othello is not without justification at
least for his confidence. He has not broken the letter of the

law. He has married Desdemona legally, by her own consent and within the auspices of the church. The senate, therefore, he knows must protect him, and he maintains a noble and imposing righteousness, all the more impressive when those around him are in turmoil. Yet, to wish to be judged, as he does, in terms of the law alone is also surely to tempt providence with self-righteousness. The total attitude which we see in Othello, insisting however confidently on justice and the law, and relying for vindication on a good reputation among men, certainly courts the condition we have described.

The influence which Othello allows the acclaim of men to exert upon him is of course not confined to this single instance. It can be traced throughout the play as a motif [theme] which is of singular importance for the interpretation of the career of Othello as tragic hero. Even in the account of the courtship in the first act we find Othello winning Desdemona by accounts of his military prowess, by stories of "battles, sieges, fortunes" (1.3.130), of "moving accidents by flood and field" (1.3.135). Two lines near the end of this famous courtship speech encapsulate its real significance:

> She lov'd me for the dangers I had pass'd,
> And I lov'd her that she did pity them. (1.3.167–68)

Judging from these lines, Othello's love for his wife would seem to be based on her acclaim of his military reputation, and there is no attempt by Othello to offset this by referring his love, on the model of good fame, to God.

FORTUNE AND HER SISTER FAME

This argument does not at all imply, however, that Shakespeare makes of Othello a simple cardboard representation of the wrong kind of fame. Hardly. The speech we are discussing is one of the most compelling and beautiful in the play, and even the Duke remarks on hearing it, "I think this tale would win my daughter, too" (1.3.171). But while critics are often content to suggest that the naive, splendid, and magniloquent Othello has married idealistically for love despite convention, and that we should feel sympathetic to such affirmation of romanticism, we might suggest a modification, rather than a cancellation of this view. Othello's poetry is of course admirable, as is his composure in face of the abuse he endures. We do indeed find ourselves hoping that things will work out well for him. But there is already, if we have eyes to see it, too much evidence that they will not. Even from the beginning we can detect in Othello a foolishness as well as merely a naivete, and what is more disconcerting, there is a certain blindness to this foolishness. Othello not only flaunts convention; he does so for the wrong reasons. His self-esteem as a man of reputation invites him to a love relationship that can only be described as uncarefully meditated. But for the moment fortune and her sister fame are conspiring in his favour.

Other places where Othello invokes reputation may now come to mind. In his explanation of why he desires Desdemona to accompany him to Cyprus, the overwhelming insistence of Othello's argument is that his reputation as a soldier will not be impaired by her presence, and the Duke should therefore give his assent:

> And heaven defend your good souls that you think
> I will your serious and great business scant,
> For she is with me; . . . no, when light-wing'd toys,
> And feather'd Cupid, foils with wanton dullness
> My speculative and active instruments,
> That my disports corrupt and taint my business,
> Let housewives make a skillet of my helm,
> And all indign and base adversities
> Make head against my reputation! (1.3.266–74)

From the beginning Othello sees love and marriage as readily imbued with implications for fame and reputation.

Again, when Cassio is cashiered [demoted in rank] we learn from Emilia that Othello will not hear a suit because:

> the Moor replies,
> That he you hurt is of great fame in Cyprus,
> And great affinity, and that in wholesome wisdom
> He might not but refuse you. (3.1.45–48)

Othello will not hear Cassio, it appears, because the injured Montano is a man of reputation of "great fame," and no doubt for Othello to commiserate with Cassio in such circumstances would be to jeopardize the integrity of his own reputation. Not only do we suspect Othello of some expediency here, but there can be no clearer example of the dangers of bad fame. For had Othello refused to let this expediency overrule mercy, and concern for reputation overrule charity, had he given Cassio a hearing, he would have protected himself against the plot which destroyed him.

His Self-esteem

Reputation once more becomes a central issue when Othello becomes convinced that he has lost Desdemona:

O now for ever
Farewell the tranquil mind, farewell content:
Farewell the plumed troop, and the big wars,
That makes ambition virtue: O farewell,
Farewell the neighing steed, and the shrill trump,
The spirit-stirring drum, the ear-piercing fife;
The royal banner, and all quality,
Pride, pomp, and circumstance of glorious war!
. . . .
Farewell, Othello's occupation's gone! (3.3.353–63)

Why Othello's occupation should be so irrevocably destroyed by his wife's supposed adultery is hard to see, except in terms of the fact that his love of his wife is bound up in an unfortunate manner with his self-esteem as a man of reputation. It is worth noting here that Iago detects this too. As he drives Othello towards the outburst we have just cited, he is careful to torment the Moor with suggestions of the painful consequences of the loss of good name among men:

Good name in man and woman, dear my lord;
Is the immediate jewel of our souls:
Who steals my purse, steals trash, 'tis something, nothing,
'Twas mine, 'tis his, and has been slave to thousands:
But he that filches from me my good name
Robs me of that which not enriches him,
And makes me poor indeed. (3.3.159–65)

Finally, as we have seen, even as he dies Othello's mind returns to reputation. Perhaps we may say in consequence he does not ever recognize the whole truth about the error of his ways, and in the last folly of his suicide, when he cannot see any hope for himself of the mercy he denied both Cassio and Desdemona, we discover the real tragedy of the story.

Fortune's Fool

Duped into believing his wife a whore, agonized by the thought of his fame destroyed in the eyes of men, Othello the "old man" so rigorous in his application of the law, is led by his "ancient" to insist on justice. But it is a perverted justice he seeks, neither informed by wisdom (*sapientia*) nor tempered by mercy, but based on the abuse of passion and supported by specious evidence interpreted by the logic of reason (*scientia*). From this pursuit only chaos can ensue. So Othello's heart is hardened. He shuts himself off from wisdom, love, good fame, and murders his wife. He becomes fortune's fool, prey to circumstance, and to the tyranny of his own passions. His human nature is perverted, and he is reduced to incoherency as his noble poetry is debased by gross and bestial language, until finally he cuts himself off from salvation by the crime of self-murder.

As the play ends, Othello comes to recognize himself as fortune's fool (5.2.324) but his recognition serves only to emphasize the enormity of his final crime. He takes his own life, not overwrought and deprived of the use of his faculties, but calmly, and with knowledge of the circumstances of his act. To the end he maintains his crucial and mistaken allegiance to bad fame. He sees himself, ironically, as one who loved "not wisely, but too well," never appreciating that one cannot love well without wisdom. So his last request involves the future of a reputation which he will not live to see traduced. His death is moving, perhaps even noble. But these emotions we must temper with pity, that such a potentially great soul should be led to such foolishness, dying, as it were, by his own knife.

Othello's Recurring Need to Role-Play

Thomas F. Van Laan

This perceptive analysis of *Othello* is by Thomas Van Laan, a veteran of the Department of English at Rutgers University. He examines the recurring theme of role-playing, in the sense that various characters take on the traits and speech of or liken themselves to certain character types. For example, in hatching his devious plot against the Moor, Iago consistently plays the part of the "honest friend," when he is anything but that. It is the title character, however, says Van Laan, who takes on many different stock roles in the course of the action, including warrior, lover, cuckold (a man with an unfaithful wife), avenger, the "malignant Turk," and the hero who kills the Turk.

Othello's involvement with role-playing is explicitly signalled quite early, in the first scene he appears in, when he prevents the battle between Brabantio's men and his own:

> Hold your hands,
> Both you of my inclining and the rest.
> Were it my cue to fight, I should have known it
> Without a prompter. (1.2.81–4)

The imagery of cue and prompter, which the role-playing of Iago in the opening scene should help to stress, identifies Othello as an actor whose part is that of the warrior. But the imagery has more importance for the service it provides in helping the spectator to perceive and place certain prominent qualities in the language of Othello's other speeches from this and, especially, the following scene. Othello is very much aware of his merits—'My parts, my title, and my perfect soul' (31)—and does not hesitate to talk about them, to celebrate them even.

There is, moreover, an extreme carefulness in his manner, which manifests itself most noticeably in his speech to the Duke and the Senators in 1.3.

Unlike Brabantio, Othello does not simply speak but delivers an oration. Brabantio is governed by the emotional upset he feels, while Othello seems excessively attentive to his audience—'Most potent, grave, and reverend signiors, / My very noble and approv'd good masters' (1.3.76–7)—and excessively concerned with constructing a specific impression of himself as one too 'rude' of speech to defend himself effectively because he has spent most of his life 'in the tented field':

> And little of this great world can I speak
> More than pertains to feats of broil and battle;
> And therefore little shall I grace my cause
> In speaking for myself. Yet, by your gracious patience,
> I will a round unvarnish'd tale deliver
> Of my whole course of love. (81–91)

This is, of course, a standard trick of the clever orator (Antony uses it in *Julius Caesar*), and therefore a more important indication of Othello's attempt to control his audience's impression of him is the shrewd way he manages to dramatize his heroic, exotic, and moving life while reporting that he had won Desdemona by dramatizing it. . . .

Othello's careful, controlled presentation of himself as meritorious is neither play-acting nor discrepant role-playing, but it is touched by both. His position in Venice and the Duke's response to him indicate that his dignity is deserved, yet he wears it in a highly histrionic [dramatic] fashion. He consciously plays himself by acting out his dignity and meritoriousness. There is, of course, a clearly recognizable explanation for this behaviour in his immediate situation. He feels defensive from the very beginning, knowing, even before Iago warns him, that he will have to cope with Brabantio's attempts to undo his marriage and perhaps destroy his career. Nevertheless, this Othello is the one Shakespeare introduces the spectators to; they may very well perceive a reason for the histrionic manner, but they cannot think of Othello apart from it. The tendency to theatricalize thus seems a fundamental part of his nature, one that his immediate situation does not create but merely renders especially visible.

Colored by Self-Doubts

Othello's tendency to act his own identity suggests his particular enjoyment of it. It is as if he were especially pleased with himself, not only for having won Desdemona from all the curled dandies of Venice but also because of his social position and the importance it lends him. There is also, however, another possible explanation for his tendency. By playing his own identity, he evokes the notion of a felt discrepancy, of a felt lack of full equivalence between this identity and himself. The impression conveyed is that he harbours doubts about whether he actually deserves this identity or whether it genuinely expresses him; and he overplays it, apparently, in order to help convince himself and others of its validity.

I am suggesting, in other words, that Othello's defensiveness does not pertain only to his worry about Brabantio but colours his entire relationship with the world outside himself. He is, as it were, unsteady on his own feet and in need of strong supports to keep him from toppling, supports like the Duke and, especially, Desdemona. The fact that he has won her provides him with his surest justification, not only because of what she signifies but because he is so certain of her love. He knows he can rely on her, and so he comes to depend on this reliance, to depend wholly upon it: 'My life upon her faith!' (1.3.294); 'Excellent wretch! Perdition catch my soul / But I do love thee; and when I love thee not / Chaos is come again' (3.3.91–3). She is, he says, the place

> where I have garner'd up my heart,
> Where either I must live or bear no life,
> The fountain from the which my current runs,
> Or else dries up. (4.2.58–61)

His 'Chaos is come again' is especially suggestive because although he apparently means the primeval chaos, his words can also denote a more personal chaos whose recurrence—or perhaps first encroachment—he deeply fears. His love for Desdemona, at any rate, is his guarantee of personal order. Should anything cause him to stop loving her, all his supports will collapse along with this supreme one, and his location in the universe will be utterly eliminated.

IAGO AN ACCOMPLISHED PLAY-MAKER

Othello's somewhat precarious situation, despite the histrionic aura he gives it, scarcely qualifies as a play of the sort Romeo and Juliet or Claudius [the king in *Hamlet*] devise, but he too must confront a counter-action consisting of a play engineered by another. The extreme contrast between Othello and Iago also extends to their histrionic activity, for where Othello's play-acting is moderate, perhaps not fully conscious, and designed to preserve, Iago's is destructive in intention, highly calculated, and constantly operative whenever he is in the presence of another. Iago, whose credo reads 'I am not what I am' (1.1.66), is a worthy successor of Richard III, and only in his soliloquies or under the cover of darkness does he say or do anything not suiting his fictitious role of 'honest Iago.' Like Richard, he is also an accomplished playmaker, as he demonstrates at once in the opening scene by shaping, with Roderigo's carefully coached assistance, the scene of disorder that sends Brabantio in search of Othello. This episode also serves as a prologue or opening scene for the primary play Iago directs against Othello. This one, which the spectators can see gradually taking shape in Iago's mind from soliloquy to soliloquy, betrays its play-like qualities most obviously in 4.1, when Iago manipulates Cassio and Bianca like puppets while Othello forms an audience of one as well as an unsuspecting participant. . . .

Iago's manipulation of Othello includes persuading him to avenge the crime Desdemona has, he thinks, committed against him, but the success of Iago's play is already assured before that, as soon as he manages to dislodge Othello from the identity he has worked so hard to keep. In addition to persuading Othello to accept the role of cuckold, Iago also, with uncanny perceptiveness, seeks to increase the sense of dislocation Othello has betrayed. He helps Othello build his feeling of being a man out of place, a Moor *in* Venice, by suggesting that Othello trusts his wife only because he does not, like Iago, sufficiently know 'our country disposition' (3.3.205) and by reminding Othello how much he differs in appearance from the native Venetians. Minutes later, after Iago has left him alone, Othello seizes upon these insinuations and adds to them, shaping the whole into a declaration of his unfitness for the role of lover:

> Haply, for I am black
> And have not those soft parts of conversation
> That chamberers have, or for I am declin'd
> Into the vale of years—yet that's not much—
> She's gone. (267–71)

Othello's acceptance of himself as cuckold destroys for him the role he has selected for his main one, that of the lover, and because he has come to depend so much on his relation to Desdemona, he loses as well his other roles, primarily his role of Venice's highly valued general. His discovery that his wife has cuckolded him becomes his cue for bidding 'Farewell' not only to 'the tranquil mind' and 'content'—and thereby further showing his increasing sense of dislocation —but also to 'the plumed troops, and the big wars / That makes ambition virtue': 'Othello's occupation's gone' (352-4, 361). For one brief moment, moreover, Othello even has an inkling of being cast adrift in a universe without meaning and clarity. He rapidly approaches full belief in Iago's lies and insinuations, but at one point he can still cry out, 'I think my wife be honest, and think she is not; / I think that thou art just, and think thou art not' (388-9).

TRYING TO ELUDE THE VOID

Two moments in 4.1 mark the climax of Othello's complete loss of identity. The more verbally explicit of these is Lodovico's expression of shock after seeing Othello strike Desdemona:

> Is this the noble Moor whom our full Senate
> Call all in all sufficient? Is this the nature
> Whom passion could not shake, whose solid virtue
> The shot of accident nor dart of chance
> Could neither graze nor pierce?

'He is much chang'd,' Iago replies (4.1.261-5). The true climax has already occurred, however, and consists of what Iago calls Othello's 'fit': the momentary total collapse marked by Othello's almost incoherent 'Lie with her—lie on her?' speech (37-44), which reflects the incoherence of his now crumbled self, and by his falling into a trance. This speech is far more than a jealous rage. It proves that Othello has seen the utter nothingness . . . the void without bearings into which loss of identity precipitately leads. Othello does not . . . try to describe or even name it, but he enacts his contact with it through his speech, and the impact it has on him is amply testified to by his loss of consciousness.

Othello can [not] bear the glimpse of nothingness . . . and find some form of response to protect himself from it. Encouraged by Iago, one of the responses he adopts is that of violence. He decides to kill the woman who has undermined his identity by making his role of lover impossible to play. He seeks to preserve himself by destroying what threatens him. He also adopts, however, another response, one with greater dramatic potential because of the abundance and variety of episodes it promises, and with richer tragic significance because it constantly dramatizes the nearness of the void and the greatness of the effort required to elude it. . . .

DRAMATIZING DESDEMONA AS A WHORE

Lines like 'I have a pain upon my forehead here' (3.3.288) and pieces of business like the examination of Desdemona's 'moist' hand (3.4.30–44) reflect Othello's attempt to play the role of cuckold, to turn it into a vehicle for preserving an ordered relationship with his surroundings. Simply adopting some of the appropriate gestures of this role does not prove entirely satisfying to him, however; his histrionic nature in conjunction with his feeling of desperate need prompts him to seek further roles and thus to shape the great role-playing episode of 4.2, in which he tries to restore certainty to his existence by concretely dramatizing the version of it that Iago has depicted for him.

Despite Emilia's insistence that Desdemona is 'honest, chaste, and true' (4.2.17), Othello must think of her as a 'subtle whore' (21), and of Emilia, accordingly, as a 'bawd' (20). Consequently, when Emilia returns with Desdemona, he addresses to Emilia a speech that assigns all three of them their appropriate roles in his little playlet:

> Some of your function, mistress:
> Leave procreants alone, and shut the door,
> Cough, or cry hem, if any body come.
> Your mystery, your mystery; nay, dispatch. (27–30)

His own role quickly alters, for with Emilia gone he plays Desdemona's accuser rather than her client. He is too grieved and angry, too outraged over what has been done to him, to be able to keep his mind focused on the *artistic* elaboration of his fiction, and so his dramatization of her as 'whore' consists for the most part merely of his frequent uses of the title (73, 87, 90) or of variations like 'public commoner' (74) and 'strumpet' (83). But as he brings the episode to a close, he resumes full dramatization, introducing this time a new twist designed to give his domestic tragedy cosmic dimensions.

As a whore protesting her innocence, Desdemona is in Othello's eyes 'double-damn'd' (38), as 'false as hell' (40). He therefore appropriately comes to experience her setting, the space she occupies, not only as brothel but also as hell itself. The two conceptions receive simultaneous dramatization when Othello ends the episode by calling Emilia back:

> You, mistress,
> That have the office opposite to Saint Peter
> And keeps the gate of hell! You, you, ay you!
> We ha done our course; there's money for your pains.
> I pray you turn the key, and keep our counsel. (91–5).

His fantasy about visiting hell has probably also an important overtone in his mind. Desdemona the whore has not merely damned herself, she has wrecked his paradise and destroyed the order of his universe; of course her location is hell because she herself is Satan. And Othello, in consequence, is a retreating, defeated Christ whose new effort to harrow hell has proved to be in vain.

AN ALIEN UNIVERSE

Othello's need for substitute roles also prompts him to give appropriate dramatic expression to his decision to kill Desdemona. The highly ritualistic ceremony in which he vows revenge characterizes his decision as the assumption of a role. He adopts the language proper to the role of avenger when he calls upon 'black vengeance' to arise 'from the hollow hell' (3.3.451) and when he sounds his cry of 'blood, blood, blood!' (455). His declaration that his 'bloody thoughts, with violent pace, / Shall ne'er look back, ne'er ebb to humble love, / Till that a capable and wide revenge / Swallow them up' (461–4) recalls Hamlet's vow to 'sweep' to his revenge—though not, I think, because Shakespeare wants his spectators to recall *Hamlet* specifically at this point, but for the reason that he regards such a claim as an example of the kind of speech that the role of avenger appropriately calls for.

Othello assumes this role, but he does not remain satisfied with its conventional formulation. Perhaps its primary move, that of delaying, of biding one's time while awaiting an almost heaven-sent opportunity, strikes him as undesirable. Perhaps he regards the standard version of the revenger's role as beneath his dignity. At any rate, with Iago's prompting, he hastens the moment of consummating his revenge, and when he approaches Desdemona's bed, he comes not as the outraged husband or the honour-offended revenger but in a new role, that of sacrificing priest, or of the God of vengeance himself. Prompted by 'the cause' (5.2.1, 3) and knowing that 'she must die, else she'll betray more men' (6), he sees himself as figuratively wielding a sword of justice (17). He cannot emulate the God of creation by re-illuming Desdemona's light once he has put it out, but he is at least godlike in his grief: 'This sorrow's heavenly; / It strikes where it doth love' (21–2). And again and again, before he kills her, he plays the priest by urging her to pray, to think on her sins, to prepare her spirit for death.

The murder of Desdemona constitutes an appropriate act for the victim of the whore-devil as well as a necessary one for the avenging god-priest, but even though the murder thus helps Othello fulfil his substitute roles, it by no means gives him peace of mind. Almost immediately, he experiences his most acute sensation of dislocated reality yet:

> My wife! my wife! what wife? I have no wife.
> O insupportable! O heavy hour!
> Methinks it should be now a huge eclipse
> Of sun and moon, and that th' affrighted globe
> Did yawn at alteration. (5.2.100–4)

The slight glimpse he once had of a disordered universe has now developed into a full, terrifying vision. And when he learns that he has fallen for Iago's lies, that it is not Desdemona but Iago and (far worse) himself who must bear the blame for destroying the perfect situation he once enjoyed, the vision takes full hold of him. More than once, he fears his own damnation, but he cannot constantly remain sure even of this horrible certainty, and his prevailing sense of the universe he now inhabits is more accurately reflected when he wonders why something so evil as Iago has not been destroyed—'Are there no stones in heaven but what serves for the thunder?' (237–8)—when he searches in vain for Iago's cloven hooves—'I look down towards his feet—but that's a fable' (289)—and when he asks the supremely tragic question his experience as a whole has forced to his lips: 'Who can control his fate?' (268). The man who had once felt out of place in his local environment, who had known what it means to be a Moor *in* Venice, now experiences the sense of dislocation appropriate to all men, which comes from inhabiting an alien universe, whose dimensions, if any, are utterly imperceptible.

OTHELLO THE MURDERER

Thus deprived of the most important bearings of all, Othello must necessarily be more concerned with what has happened to him than with what he has done. He feels remorse for having killed Desdemona and some grief because she is dead, but mainly he dwells on the vulnerability he has acquired by his crime. Not only has he lost Desdemona for all eternity, but through this act he has also cancelled out for

ever the other pillar of his identity, his original role as
Othello the valiant hero:

> I am not valiant neither—
> But every puny whipster gets my sword.
> But why should honour outlive honesty?
> Let it go all. (246–9)

Desperately, he tries to hang on to this role, by mentioning,
even though alone, the special nature of the sword he still
has access to:

> I have another weapon in this chamber;
> It was a sword of Spain, the ice-brook's temper (255–6). . . .

The seemingly excessive egotism Othello manifests in this
scene, as well as earlier, is not, I think, primarily a quality of
his own individuality. . . . The great self-concern may well be
inevitable in the basic Shakespearian tragic situation. Loss
of identity means that the ties linking one to others have already been severed; there remains, in effect, no one for the
victim of identity loss to be concerned with outside himself.
And even if there were, the state of identity loss—or, more
accurately, the consciousness of this loss and of the abyss
that opens before one—creates such a desperate need to
struggle for self-preservation that thought of anyone or anything else borders on the impossible.

Othello's final act affirms once more and decisively the
kind of need the tragic situation produces. The speech beginning 'Soft you; a word or two before you go' (341) shows
once again the oratorical grace and the careful, studied presentation of a self Othello had exhibited in his speech to the
Duke and Senators. Then he felt his identity threatened and
sought to solidify it through his performance; now he seeks
to re-create an identity where none any longer exists and
thus preserve himself from the encroaching nothingness.
The identity Othello here acts out is his old one. He is once
again the valiant hero who has 'done the state some service'
(342), and he is also the lover, albeit one that 'lov'd not
wisely, but too well' (347) and that, as a result, must accus-
tom his eyes to 'the melting mood' (352). His earlier efforts
to re-establish his role as Othello the hero failed because he
could not effectively supplement his words with the proper
gestures and moves. Now, however, he validates his words
through two highly appropriate emblematic gestures (the
sword thrust and the kiss); and through his death, he makes
sure that contradictory external circumstances cannot mock

his performance. Othello the murderer has been absorbed into the 'malignant' Turk, which is only one of the roles Othello now plays. He dies as the malignant Turk, but he also dies as the hero who smote him; and as Desdemona's true and faithful lover, he dies 'upon a kiss' (362). The three roles of malignant Turk, hero, and lover all validly represent aspects of Othello's experience; the necessity of their being maintained through histrionic effort and the fact that this effort constitutes a willed alternative to the perception of nothingness bespeak the thoroughness with which this experience has been a tragic one.

CHAPTER 4

Major Modern Stage and Film Adaptations of the Play

READINGS ON
OTHELLO

Orson Welles Produces *Othello* on a Shoestring

Roger Manvell

One of the most famous film adaptations of Shakespeare's *Othello* was the 1955 version, directed by and
starring the controversial American actor-producer-
director Orson Welles. By the time he began shooting
the film, Welles already had a reputation in Hollywood as both a genius and an arrogant financial
risk, and he had a great deal of trouble raising the
funds to make *Othello.* The result was a shoestring
budget and a long, chaotic, on-again-off-again shooting schedule, factors which ended up marring, to
one degree or another, the film's visual and auditory
qualities. In this frank review from his highly regarded book *Shakespeare and the Film,* Roger Manvell, former head of the Department of Film History
at the London Film School, describes the production's problems. Manvell also points out that, despite
the low budget, Welles managed to create some stun-
ning visual images and, in Manvell's opinion, ended
up with a better Shakespearean adaptation than his
earlier film of *Macbeth* (also shot on a very low budget). What makes this and other film versions of
Shakespeare's plays important and fascinating, re-
gardless of their qualities or successes as movies, is
the way that new generations of artists freshly interpret the plays, imparting new twists and making
them relevant for diverse ages and societies.

Plans for the film of *Othello* followed Welles's removal to Europe. Peter Noble, in *The Fabulous Orson Welles,* gives a sum-
mary account of the vicissitudes through which this film
passed, including reshooting to cover three successive Desdemonas (Lea Padovani, Betsy Blair and Suzanne Cloutier).

Excerpted from Roger Manvell, *Shakespeare and the Film* (New York: A.S. Barnes,
1979). Copyright 1971, 1979 by Roger Manvell.

In all, it took from 1949 to 1952 to complete the film in successive phases, filming in Rome, Morocco (Mogador, Safi and Mazagram) and Italy (Venice, Tuscany, Rome, Viterbo, Perugia). From the actors' point of view, Micheál MacLiammóir, who played Iago, published a diary of his experiences, *Put Money in Thy Purse*, which is as entertaining as it is revealing. Welles had constantly to abandon work on the film and acquire more money either from backers or from his own considerable earnings starring in other people's productions. The film was finally released in 1955, reaching Britain the following year.

THE STUNNING OPENING SCENE

Like *Macbeth*, *Othello* has a magnificent visual flair, stemming this time not from studio sets but from a brilliant use of the locations. Welles imposed no new or artificial interpretation on the play, as he had done so disastrously in the case of *Macbeth*; rather, he widened its environment by using Italian and Moroccan backgrounds, especially the battlements of the eighteenth-century Arab citadel at Mogador. I first saw the opening reel when Welles himself presented it during a lecture at the Edinburgh Film Festival in 1953. It begins with the upturned face of the dead Othello in the funeral cortège he shares with Desdemona. The deeply vibrating notes of a choral dirge accompanied by powerful piano chords resound as the procession of figures cowled in black moves forward on the battlements, silhouetted against the skyline. Below are the watching crowds. Suddenly Iago is hustled forward past the procession, a halter round his neck, his eyes wild with fear. He is thrust into a wooden cage and winched upwards to the top of the walls, swinging, staring down at his tormentors, and at the funeral procession of the man and woman whose deaths he has caused. The music has grown now into harsh chords echoed by the clanging of bells.

Only after this come the opening titles, and the narration spoken by Orson Welles about the subject of the film, followed by the relatively hurried scenes in Venice before the action takes Othello and Desdemona to Cyprus. It is unfortunate that once again the sound recording is so ill-balanced that the speech is often barely intelligible. The characterization, however, is better balanced than in *Macbeth*; in his old friend, MacLiammóir, Welles had an actor worthy to play opposite him; and Fay Compton made a strong Emilia.

WELLES'S CONCEPTION OF DESDEMONA

In this excerpt from her book Othello: A Contextual History, *Clark University scholar Virginia M. Vaughan explains how Welles portrayed Desdemona as "the passive object of male fantasies and desire."*

Welles first displays Othello's face (upside down) upon a funeral bier that is slowly carried along the top of the fortress walls. A procession of monks follows the body, holding a cross aloft. The camera lingers next over the pale face of Desdemona under a transparent shroud. As her bier passes, the camera shifts first to Iago, who gazes down upon her body from the cage where he has been hoisted; then we see the faces of her male countrymen, Lodovico and Cassio, who might have been her lovers but were not. They cross themselves as they watch her body pass. Even before the film's title appears, Desdemona is represented in all her *to-be-looked-at-ness* as a silent, inert body, the passive object of male fantasies and desires.

Iago also studies Othello's corpse from his lofty cage. Thus from the film's opening shots we have Desdemona and Othello identified as what film critic Judith Mayne describes as sites of "ambivalent positions of desire." Desdemona's body, repeatedly serves as the locus for Othello's desire, while Iago's gaze is directed at Othello and fraught with homoerotic overtones.

Images of Desdemona's body repeat throughout the film. Aroused from her marital bed after the drunken brawl, for example, Desdemona appears aloft in a shining, white dress. As she descends to Othello's side, the camera pans to the men assembled about her, and in a reverse angle shot we see what she would see, a host of men staring at her. Once the temptation begins, she appears in bright sunlight on the battlements, and then the camera jumps to a darkened Othello below, gazing up at her. Light haloes from her face when she speaks for Cassio. Later in the same sequence, after she realizes something is wrong with Othello, her figure is again highlighted in whiteness. . . . A small speck of white space between two dark, phallic pillars, Desdemona physically represents the object of male anxiety, the emptiness that must be filled, the force that must be chained.

Virginia M. Vaughan, *Othello: A Contextual History.* New York: Cambridge University Press, 1994, pp. 207–208.

Suzanne Cloutier, however, had little to offer but her looks for Desdemona, whom she tries to play with youthful spirit. MacLiammóir gives Iago a coldly cerebral villainy; he is a quiet-spoken, Elizabethan Machiavel [villain], who knows how to set about his business. 'I hate the Moor,' he says to Roderigo, at the very beginning of the action in Venice. The temptation scenes, therefore, are effectively played, and had the recording been clearer there is no doubt that the characterization would appear even more detailed and effective than it does with the words sometimes scarcely audible. There is one striking shot, a single long take on the battlements using a jeep to achieve a tracking shot as Iago, walking beside Othello, first rouses suspicion in him as to Cassio's intentions with Desdemona.

TOO MUCH PHOTOGRAPHIC BEAUTY?

Once again, Welles lends his large, theatrical personality to the part of Othello. Peter Cowie, in *The Cinema of Orson Welles*, claims there are some five hundred shots in the film, which runs only ninety-one minutes, and that in consequence the montage is extremely fragmented; the use of dissolves is frequent since appropriate shots were not always there for direct cutting. Again, Welles cut deep into the text of the play, isolating the dialogue and speeches he needed in order to carry the action forward, transposing when he felt the urge. A brilliant touch of improvisation, celebrated by now, was the resetting of the scene in which Roderigo (after plotting Cassio's murder, with Iago) is himself murdered by Iago; Welles decided to film this in a Turkish bath because the costumes for Cassio and Roderigo were not available at the times of shooting. The result is one of the most effective scenes in the film, with Roderigo stabbed by Iago as he hides under the slatted boards in the Turkish bath, surrounded by clouds of steam.

However, the large number of strikingly lit architectural shots coming in quick succession on the screen makes the film restless, and to this extent more difficult to enter into. . . . So much photographic beauty becomes a drug. The characters move rapidly, and the camera is tilted upwards to the point of obsession. . . . In the beginning, Iago and Roderigo, seldom still, watch Othello's movements, now in the Ca' d'Oro in Venice (which becomes Brabantio's house), now from the balconies surrounding the courtyard of the

Doge's Palace. The film is at its best when this restlessness
is broken and a certain degree of concentration is allowed—
when Othello addresses the Doge, for example, with his
story of how he wooed Desdemona, who stands listening in
the doorway, still rapt in wonder, and joins him to confront
her father and the Doge as he concludes the speech. Most of
this is covered in close shot. Some of the later interchanges
between Iago and Othello are fragmented into a series of
emphatically tilted portraits, which drain the drama from
the speech, which is in any case under-emphasized, and so
transform the scenes into a photographic exhibition. A similar beauty destroys, not enhances, the intensity of the later
scenes between Othello and Desdemona, which are posed in
a succession of beautiful architectural interiors. The music,
too, though often apt, is sometimes used in such a way as to
prove a further distraction, disintegrating the dramatic effect. This is particularly so when it is used cacophonously,
out of tune, at the moment Othello leaves Iago and launches
his first jealous suspicion directly at Desdemona. The music
becomes then inordinately emphatic—huge chords resound
as Othello's jealous imagination seizes on the image of Desdemona's adultery—'lie with her, on her—'. Suddenly the
seagulls are seen wheeling in the sky, and Othello is lying
on his back in a fit. Choral music breaks in on Othello's
laments for Desdemona's beauty—'She might lie by an Em-
peror's side—'.

A PLAY OF DARKNESS

Cutting is often used to great effect. When Othello strikes
Desdemona in front of the delegation from Venice, the blow
is struck in a straight cut, and is as effective as it is startling
and horrifying. In its own way, the scene leading up to the
suffocating of Desdemona is effective—Othello, in close
shot, pinches out the candle, the contours of his face revealed in highlights against the blackout, his eyes concentrated. It is a play of darkness rather than light. When Desdemona dies, her face is seen faintly outlined beneath the
thin veils of the fine cloth that suffocates her. The film ends
as it began, with the funeral procession, the chanting, and
the dead face of Othello.

An Inventive Russian Film Captures *Othello*'s Moral Center

Derek Prouse

While American actor-director Orson Welles was making his version of *Othello* in the late 1940s and early 1950s, the acclaimed Russian film director Sergei Youtkevich was preparing his own adaptation of the play. Released in 1955, Youtkevich's version is not only visually beautiful, but demonstrates that even when Shakespeare's words are translated into another language, the characters and story can still be moving and effective. Less concerned with the language than the visuals, Youtkevich was free to concentrate on finding and capturing the human drama in cinematic terms; as explained in this perceptive 1956 review by noted film critic Derek Prouse, he was particularly successful in emphasizing the moral implications of Othello's fall from grace.

Sergei Youtkevich has defined his interpretation of Othello's tragedy not primarily as one of love and jealousy but of misplaced trust. Othello's murderous act is committed in defence of truth and justice, out of the violation of his faith in man's noble and harmonious destiny. For many years Youtkevich has cherished his dream of bringing *Othello* to the screen . . . and now the final result, meaningful and mature, carries the weight of a subject profoundly felt and understood.

A DISTURBING FATALISM

The first quality that strikes one in the film is the authority and confident ease with which it takes to the open air. Here is no calculated transference of a stage classic to the screen,

Reprinted from Derek Prouse, *"Othello," Sight and Sound*, vol. 26, no. 1 (Summer 1956).

but a total reconsideration of the subject from first to last in terms of cinema.

Othello himself is first seen through the eyes of Desdemona. She spins an ornamental globe dreamily, and the scene fades. We see Othello, hero of the countless exploits which have fired her romantic imagination—the valiant warrior, the shipwrecked galley slave, the natural candidate for the highest honour and renown. The dream fades . . . into the credit titles. (Welles' pre-credits action was the funeral cortege; "He began with death, I began with life," Youtkevich is reported impartially to have observed. . . .) We next see Othello in his time of full contentment. His noble conception of life has proved an attainable ideal. To Desdemona he is the tenderest of lovers, and in the Senate he speaks from a deep, certain and rapturous self-fulfilment. After the marriage (it is Cassio who guides the swift and secret gondola along the night canal), when Brabantio strides, dismayed and angry, from the Senate, it is almost as an afterthought that he turns to hurl back his warning: "Look to her, Moor, if thou hast eyes to see; she has deceived her father, and may thee." As Othello and Desdemona move down the wide, sunlit steps to the square below, Desdemona drops her handkerchief. Iago, hovering and alert, darts forward to retrieve it and thereby to earn his first "honest Iago." A masterly ironic stroke, and a brilliantly casual strengthening of the incidents to come.

Passions, both secret and open, bind the central characters together and inform their every action. A provocative and sexually eager Emilia buys Iago's kisses rather than his good-humour with the purloined handkerchief. Her arm twists across the screen as she coquettishly teases her husband with the handkerchief; later, Othello's hand will be seen in an arresting close-up as he desperately demands the handkerchief from Desdemona. And in the final scene the same handkerchief is raised to Cassio's lips. Was Desdemona urged to plead for him by an almost unconscious awareness of his love for her? Did some psychic recognition of this in Othello render Iago's work that much the easier? By such hints and speculations the knot of central passions is slowly tightened, and by such subtle preparation as this early planting of the handkerchief coincidence is elevated to a disturbing and dramatic fatalism. Not even the willow song is avoided, despite the threat it can clearly present to realism on the screen. Youtkevich has already shown us a Desdemona who loves to sing, and the first seeds of suspicion are sown to the sound of her singing as her boat drifts across the bay. Later, when her happiness is already overshadowed, she is still heard singing sadly.

INVENTIVE DIRECTORIAL TOUCHES

The first scene of treachery is a typical example of Youtkevich's invention. A conception that, given a less than impeccable feeling for the total shape of the action, might have defied control or remained merely bleakly abstract, here amplifies the scene with a striking dramatic symbolism. As the two men walk along the beach (the same scene in Welles' film was also shot on the move), and Iago's hints assume their meaning for Othello, they pass through a tangle of fishing nets. The nets hang more densely, Othello's perturbation mounts, and physical and mental claustrophobia commingle. In their next scene together, the seeds have taken root; the treachery is already a complex growth, and a note of fearful intimacy is struck. Convinced finally of Desdemona's guilt, Othello sinks to his knees on the shore, oblivious of the waves dashing against him. Iago kneels beside him: and as Othello's head sinks on his breast, there is something of a lover's ecstasy in Iago's thrill of possessive triumph:

OTHELLO: Now art thou my lieutenant.

IAGO: I am your own forever.

There are interesting uses of soliloquy throughout *Othello*. The key speech, "O now, for ever . . . Farewell the tranquil mind" is extracted from the scene with Iago and treated as a soliloquy. Othello walks through the camp at night, speaking his distracted thoughts aloud, unaware of the amazed concern of his men. On the occasion of Othello's arrival in Cyprus, Iago is seen in close-up, backed by the festive fireworks. His thoughts are heard on the sound track but his lips . . . remain motionless. Later, Iago addresses another soliloquy to his reflection mirrored in a well. This captures effectively the quality of dramatic dialectic inherent in soliloquy, its essential function as an inner dialogue between brain and spirit. Othello also addresses his own reflection in the same pool, but here the need is for an assuagement [calming] of his torment, a desperate attempt to rediscover a remembered peace in the mirrored face.

AN AUTHENTICALLY TRAGIC HERO

I have already mentioned Youtkevich's remarkable visual sense. . . . Much of the action takes place out of doors, but the passions lose none of their intensity when exposed to the bright sunlight backed up by the blue sea. Iago is seen alone in foreground shadow while Othello is teased by a skittish Desdemona under clustering sundrenched vines; Othello reels in his first onrush of anguish against a burning white wall. It is only towards the end that the clouds gather, the candles are lighted, and the drama darkens to climax. Here [actor] Sergei Bondarchuck [in the role of Othello] rises finely to the tragedy's demands, presenting a naturally noble spirit fearfully wracked in its battle against baffling and malignant odds. After the murder, particular mention should be given to A. Maximova's Emilia. Her horrified inability to grasp the enormity of her husband's offence is a powerful and true interpretation of a challenging scene. A. Popov's Iago is a plausible villain, generally withdrawn and watchful, but enough of the extrovert to sing a lusty soldier's song at a celebration. Competent enough to serve the director's main intention, this is not, though, a performance that attains any great subtlety.

Youtkevich has defined the tragedy's climax as follows:

I believe that after the murder of Desdemona the Moor remains calm. The tragedy only attains its climax at the moment when Emilia reveals her husband's lie. . . . The treachery of "honest Iago" is what finally plunges Othello into chaos. Iago is calm; he has lost the game, but as long as Othello lives he is the victor. When Othello raises his dagger, it is Iago who leaps forward to stop him, having understood his intention. Othello's death negates the victory of Iago. The Moor pays for his crime with blood. His courage and his honesty elevate him above Iago. The final wave of Iago's envy breaks forth: he has lost the last round.

The moral implications which Youtkevich discovers in the work make his Othello an authentically tragic hero; his collapse is a disintegration from the highest spiritual refinement. And in the final scenes Othello's calm re-assumption of his lost nobility—his withdrawal from earthly chaos—lends the tragedy a deeply moving dying fall. An elevating and intensely satisfying exposition of the play, this Russian *Othello* must rank with the best of filmed Shakespeare.

Olivier's Legendary Interpretation of the Moor

Anthony Holden

England's Laurence Olivier (died 1989) is widely acknowledged as the twentieth century's foremost English-speaking actor. He is perhaps most famous for his Shakespearean parts, including the title roles in *Hamlet, Macbeth, Henry V, King Lear,* and *Othello.* He played the latter on stage in 1964 at England's National Theater, a production recorded on film the following year. This description of Olivier's assault on the role of Shakespeare's Moor is from the popular biography of the actor by noted columnist, editor, and biographer Anthony Holden. Explaining first how English theater critic Kenneth Tynan, a close friend of Olivier's, persuaded the actor to play Othello, Holden describes Olivier's controversial performance of the role as an African black. Most earlier interpretations of the role by white actors had presented Othello more as Shakespeare had intended—as a dark-skinned Moor (the product of mixed racial background), and some people thought Olivier's interpretation was a caricature of modern blacks. But as Holden makes clear, Olivier's choice of interpretation was on the one hand not meant as a caricature, and on the other ultimately overshadowed by the sheer magnificence of his performance, which one critic called "altogether unforgettable by anyone who saw it."

[Kenneth] Tynan had embarked on what he regarded as little less than a national duty: the persuading of Olivier to undertake the only major Shakespeare role he had so far, by

Excerpted from Anthony Holden, *Laurence Olivier: A Biography* (New York: Atheneum, 1988). Copyright © 1988 by Anthony Holden Ltd. Reproduced by permission of the authors c/o Rogers, Coleridge & White Ltd., 20 Powis Mews, London W11 1JN.

his own confession, funked: Othello. Tynan tried to present the idea as a *fait accompli* [accomplished fact], rightly suspecting that he would be hitting a raw nerve. Years of shouldering the mightiest Shakespearean parts had convinced Olivier that they were "cannibals":

> You give them all you've got and the author says to you: "You've given all you've got? Good. Now, more. Good. Now, more. More, damn you. More, more! *More! More!*" Until your heart and guts and brain are pulp and the part feeds on you, eating you. Acting great parts devours you. It's a dangerous game.

And Othello was the most dangerous of them all. The part was a "monstrous, monstrous burden" for any actor. "I think Shakespeare and Richard Burbage got drunk together one night and Burbage said, 'I can play anything you write, anything at all.' And Shakespeare said, 'Right, I'll fix you, boy!' And then he wrote *Othello.*" Olivier pointed out to Tynan that no English actor this century had succeeded in the part; the play really belonged to Iago, who could make the Moor look "a credulous idiot". Olivier was guiltily reminded of his own exotically Freudian Iago, which had so undermined [noted English actor] Ralph Richardson's Othello in this same theatre a quarter of a century before. "If I take it on," he told Tynan, "I don't want a witty, Machiavellian Iago. I want a solid, honest-to-God NCO [noncommissioned officer, i.e, an actor of considerably smaller reputation and stage-presence]." The notion suited John Dexter, who was eager to direct what he believed could be Olivier's greatest performance. And just the right NCO was available from the junior ranks of the company: Frank Finlay, whose only previous Shakespearean experience was a brief appearance from the waist up as the gravedigger in . . . *Hamlet.*

For a while Olivier still hesitated, though Tynan suspected that it may all have been more offstage acting: "It was not easy to persuade him to play Othello. At least, he made it seem difficult; perhaps, deep in his personal labyrinth [complex inner self], where the minotaur [monster] of his talent lurks, he had already decided and merely wanted to be coaxed." Tynan's gambit was to tackle the issue head on: "You've done all the others. People will wonder why you're ducking this one." Still Olivier protested that he was not right for the part: "I haven't got the voice, Ken," he kept saying. "Othello has to have a dark, black, violet, velvet *bass* voice." Tynan mentioned the problem to Orson Welles, who

CAPTURING THE GRANDEUR OF AFRICA

This review of Olivier's Othello, written by the New States-man*'s Ronald Bryden shortly after the production opened, perceptively observes that the actor's controversial choice of interpretation was intended to ennoble and glorify, rather than to exploit or poke fun at, the image of a larger-than-life black African warrior.*

He came on smelling a rose, laughing softly, with a private delight; barefooted, ankleted, black. He had chosen to play a Negro. . . . It could have been a caricature, an embarrassment. Instead, after the second performance, a well-known Negro actor rose in the stalls bravo-ing. For obviously it was done with love; with the main purpose of substituting for the Moorish empire one modern audiences could respond to: the grandeur of Africa. He was the continent, like a figure of Rubens's allegory. . . . The last speech was spoken kneeling on the bed, her body clutched upright to him as a shield for the dagger he turns on himself. As he *slumped* beside her on the sheets, the current stopped. A couple of wigged actors stood awkwardly about. You could only pity them: we had seen history, and it was over.

Quoted in Logan Gourlay, ed., *Olivier.* New York: Stein and Day, 1973, p. 193.

agreed: "Larry's a natural tenor, and Othello's a natural baritone." All it took was for Tynan to voice Welles's doubts to Olivier himself; he was fixed for a moment by what [English actor Peter] O'Toole had called "that grey-eyed miopic stare that can turn you to stone", and the next thing everyone knew was that the boss, after forty years in the business, was taking voice coaching. Day by day, through the plywood walls of the temporary offices, Tynan heard a throbbing, growling noise which grew ever lower and lower. With the help of Barry Smith, a voice teacher at RADA [Royal Academy of Dramatic Arts], Olivier spent six months deepening the pitch of his voice by an entire octave.

A NATURAL FORCE

The effect at the first read-through was "shattering". Into what is normally a relaxed, get-to-know-you session, at which the actors mumble their way amiably through the text, Olivier "tossed a hand grenade". Even Tynan's jaw dropped as Olivier, "seated, bespectacled and lounge-suited,

fell on the text like a tiger . . . a fantastic, full-volume display
that scorched one's ears, serving final notice on everyone present that the hero, storm-centre and focal point of this tragedy
was the man named in the title". This was not the urbane, civilized Othello of theatrical tradition, but "a triumphant black
despot, aflame with unadmitted self-regard", who even at that
reading managed the impossible trick which was to make
Olivier's Othello, for all the controversy which came to surround it, so memorable: "So far from letting Iago manipulate
him, he seemed to manipulate Iago, treating him as a kind of
court jester. Such contumely cried out for deflation."

The windows shook at the sound of Olivier's voice, and Tynan's scalp tingled: "A natural force had entered the room."
As the cast sat "pole-axed", Tynan pondered the scale of the
risk Olivier appeared to be taking this time. Might not the
"knockdown arrogance" of this interpretation be too close for
comfort to comedy? By cutting the hero down to size, dis-
pensing with his intrinsic majesty, was not Olivier doing to
Othello precisely what he had deplored about [English actor]
Paul Scofield's *King Lear* (directed by Peter Brook), which he
had witheringly taken to calling "*Mr* Lear"? Then came
"Farewell the plumed troop"—to Tynan . . . "like the dying
moan of a fighting bull"—and all reservations vanished.

> We were learning what it meant to be faced with a great clas-
> sical actor in full spate—one whose vocal range was so im-
> mense that by a single new inflexion he could point the way
> to a whole new interpretation. Every speech, for Olivier, is
> like a mass of marble at which the sculptor chips away until
> its essential force and meaning are revealed. No matter how
> ignoble the character he plays, the result is always noble as a
> work of art.

THE MAKE-UP

Olivier, having got the voice right, now decided what he
wanted to look like. His lifelong obsession with make-up
reached its apogee, as he told Dexter he thought the modern
trend towards "coffee-coloured compromise" was a "cop-out
. . . as if the Moor could not be thought a truly *noble* Moor if
he was too black, and in too great a contrast to the noble
whites". This, surely, was a "shocking case of pure snobbery".
Anxious as ever to stun, to astonish, Olivier's Othello would
overlook the genetic difference between a Moor and a negro;
he would be black with a vengeance, black as night, jet-black
as the text could justify. Did it not refer to his "thick lips", his

"sooty bosom"? Did he himself not say: "Haply for I am black," etc.? The man was a *negro*: he would look and talk and walk like a negro—yes, a contemporary negro, of the kind now commonplace (if only recently) on the streets of London. Across Waterloo Bridge, on the edge of the black ghettoes developing in the south of the capital, Olivier began to gift-wrap the most risqué of 400th birthday presents for his beloved Bard.

Olivier took two and a half hours each night to transform himself into Othello, and an hour afterwards to re-emerge. He started by covering his body from head to toe with a coat of dark stain, over which went a layer of greasy black make-up, which he and his dresser then polished vigorously with a chiffon cloth, to achieve a shiny finish—as if his body were the toecap of a giant army boot, due on the sovereign's parade. The palms of his hands, the soles of his feet, his specially thickened lips and even his tongue were then dyed with incarnadine; a course of drops added a penetrating sheen to the whites of his eyes; he even varnished his fingernails to give them a pallid blue lustre. The wig was of crinkly, matted curls, flecked with grey at the temples, and the final touch was a thin, surly-looking moustache. Most backstage anecdotes about this production concern people of either gender walking in on a naked Olivier, of various hues between Brighton white and Caribbean black, because it all had to dry before he could don Othello's pristine white robe.

A SENSE OF LEGEND-MAKING IN THE AIR

Then came the walk: a gently rolling, loose-limbed gait, swaying from the hips on naked feet, prowling around the stage with the easy, flowing movements of a giant cat. His first appearance each evening, idly toying with a red rose, his mouth smiling the most complacent of smiles, falling open to reveal a blood-red tongue, drew gasps even before his unwontedly deep, dark voice froze the theatre back into stunned silence. As Olivier stood with his feet wide apart, trunk leaning gently forwards, emphasizing his words with the palms of his hands, his arms so languid that they might have been on ball-bearings, there was a sense of theatrical history, of legend-making in the air.

"By heaven knows what witchcraft", wrote Herbert Kretzmer of the *Daily Express*, Olivier had "managed to capture the very essence of what it must mean to be born with a dark skin. . . . It is a performance full of grace, terror and inso-

lence. I shall dream of its mysteries for years to come."
Harold Hobson, too, believed that "the power, passion,
verisimilitude and pathos of Sir Laurence's performance are
things which will be spoken of with wonder for a long time
to come." Philip Hope-Wallace of the *Guardian* found that
"the inventiveness of it, the sheer variety and range of the
actor's art . . . made it an experience in the theatre altogether
unforgettable by anyone who saw it". Only Alan Brien of the
Sunday Telegraph dissented, in a vivid minority report still
remembered by those who thought that this time Olivier—
the "Creole" Othello—had gone too far:

> There is a kind of bad acting of which only a great actor is ca-
> pable. I find Sir Laurence Olivier's Othello the most prodigious
> and perverse example of this in a decade. . . . Sir Laurence is
> elaborately at ease, graceful and suave, more like a seducer
> than a cuckold. But as the jealousy is transfused into his blood,
> the white man shows through more obviously. He begins to
> double and treble his vowels, to stretch his consonants, to stag-
> ger and shake, even to vomit, near the frontiers of self-parody.
> His hips oscillate, his palms rotate, his voice skids and slides so
> that the Othello music takes on a Beatle beat.

MORE AWE THAN SYMPATHY

The physical disintegration was, in fact, deliberate. As he
prepared for the physical demands of the role, jogging along
the Brighton seafront and intensifying his daily workouts at
the gym, Olivier realized precisely why actors had always
found Othello so mountainous a challenge. The part reaches
so many climaxes, most of them (the epileptic fit, for instance) as taxing physically as vocally, that it drains the per-
former long before the climactic final scene. At the age of
fifty-seven, the only way Olivier could pace himself through
its rigours was to let go of the immense, physical discipline
he imposed on himself in the early scenes. As Iago's poison
did its work, this Othello would go to pieces bodily as much
as emotionally. Olivier did not spare the audience with his
final collapse, tearing the crucifix from around his neck, and
wailing hopelessly to the pagan gods from which baptism
had supposedly delivered him—returning, on "O the pity of
it, Iago," to the atavism of his true, ancestral past. For a hero
whose tragic flaws had been so vividly drawn, the spectator
felt less sympathy than awe. Here, as Olivier finally pulled
off a mercurial, almost magic-trick suicide, was a death to
inspire pity and terror rather than tears.

It was but one aspect of the production which sparked a debate lasting to this day. Given so towering a central performance, and the ego of the actor giving it, did Iago really have to become so doltish a lump as poor Frank Finlay was obliged to portray?. . . Left to his own devices, Finlay's Iago became an unconvincing, inconsistent rogue, his crime more than ever out of proportion to his grievance. Only when dealing directly with Othello—thanks also to the fact that Olivier was always at his best when in close tactile contact with another actor or actress—did Finlay really come into his own. In the latter stages of the play, as Olivier's Othello began to disintegrate, Finlay's Iago clung about his neck—"almost", as one critic put it, "with the embrace of a succubus", pouring poison into his ear "in tones of satanic lullaby".

RACE RELATIONS

Olivier's stunningly vivid negro also drew the play, more directly than was entirely comfortable, into the embattled contemporary arena of race relations. It was not just that Olivier's Moor belonged more to the Caribbean than to Cyprus. . . . In the 1960s, Hobson reluctantly accepted, it would have been "unrealistic" to expect Iago, a motiveless persecutor of a black man, to be portrayed as a person of high, if malicious, intelligence. But above all it was Olivier who, with the curl of his lip, the rhythmic movements of his body, the roll of his staring eyes, the uneasy mixture of arrogance and inferiority, transformed *Othello* into an urgent "world-drama" as much as a harrowing case-history of individual betrayal.

The textual argument tended to drown in controversy over Olivier's negro—an astonishing technical achievement, it was agreed, but at what price to the text? If Olivier was too much the sophisticated negro, too little the noble Moor, Shakespeare, as J.W. Lambert argued, would surely have cared little for the distinction: "But he would surely have delighted in the portrait of an alienated man, fighting against his own people, a black among whites, a soldier among civilians, a middle-aged professional with an upper-class wife." In Shakespeare, said Olivier himself,

> I always try to reassure the audience initially that they are not going to see some grotesque, outsized dimension of something which they can't understand or sympathize with. If you have succeeded in the initial moments, either by a very

strong stamp of characterization so they recognize you as a
real guy, or by a quiet approach, then I think there's no end
to where you can lead them in size of acting a little later in
the evening. God knows, you have to be enormously big as
Othello. It has to be big stuff.

Displaying a canny sense of his times, moreover, he added
with a wistful regret: "I don't know: it may be that this is a
time which refuses to look greatness full in the face. Perhaps
it will tolerate it only with an oblique look. . . ." [In fact, the-
atergoers of that time were treated to more than an oblique
look at greatness.] . . . Olivier's *Othello* had been playing for
six months before the Italian director Franco Zeffirelli saw
it: "I had been told that this was the last flourish of romantic acting. It's nothing of the sort. It's an anthology of everything that has been discovered about acting in the last three
centuries."

Chronology

1543

Polish astronomer Nicolaus Copernicus introduces the idea of a sun- rather than earth-centered universe in his *On the Revolutions*.

1557

William Shakespeare's parents, John Shakespeare and Mary Arden, are married.

1558

Elizabeth I becomes queen of England, initiating the so-called Elizabethan age.

1564

William Shakespeare is born in the village of Stratford in central England; his noted contemporary, writer Christopher Marlowe, is also born.

1566

Italian writer Giraldi Cinthio first publishes his collection of short stories, the *Hecatommithi*, from which Shakespeare will later borrow some of his plots, including that of *Othello*.

1572

Playwright Ben Jonson, later a rival of Shakespeare's, is born.

1576

London's first public theater, the Theatre, opens.

1577–1580

Englishman Sir Francis Drake sails around the world.

1582

William Shakespeare marries Anne Hathaway.

1585

Shakespeare's twins, Hamnet and Judith, are born.

1587

Queen Elizabeth executes her rival, Mary, Queen of Scots; at about this time Shakespeare leaves Stratford and heads for London to pursue a career in the theater.

1588

England wins a major victory over Spain by defeating the mighty Spanish Armada.

CA. 1590–1593

Shakespeare writes *Richard III, The Comedy of Errors, Henry VI, Parts 1, 2,* and *3,* and *Titus Andronicus.*

1593–1594

While London's theaters are closed due to an outbreak of the plague, Shakespeare writes and publishes two long poems, *Venus and Adonis* and *The Rape of Lucrece.*

1594

Shakespeare joins the newly formed Lord Chamberlain's Men theatrical company.

CA. 1594–1600

Shakespeare writes *The Taming of the Shrew, The Two Gentlemen of Verona, The Merry Wives of Windsor, Twelfth Night, Richard II, Henry IV, Parts 1* and *2, Henry V,* and *Julius Caesar.*

1597

Shakespeare buys New Place, the largest home in Stratford.

1598–1599

The Globe opens; Shakespeare owns one-eighth of its profits.

1600

In Italy, the Catholic Church burns priest Giordano Bruno at the stake for advocating the idea that the stars are other suns, each having its own planets.

1600–1601

The Moorish ambassador of the king of Barbary visits Queen Elizabeth's court, possibly providing Shakespeare with his inspiration for the physical attributes and noble character of the hero of his yet-to-be-written play *Othello.*

CA. 1601–1602

Shakespeare writes *Othello;* in the following few years he turns out other great tragedies, including *King Lear, Macbeth,* and *Antony and Cleopatra.*

1603

Queen Elizabeth dies; James I becomes king of England; the English conquer Ireland.

1607

English settlers establish the colony of Jamestown, giving England a permanent foothold in North America.

CA. **1608–1613**

Shakespeare writes *Coriolanus, The Winter's Tale, Henry VIII,* and *The Two Noble Kinsmen.*

1610

Italian scholar Galileo Galilei points his newly built telescope at the planet Jupiter and discovers four orbiting moons, proving conclusively that all heavenly bodies do not revolve around the earth.

1611

The King James Version of the Bible is published.

1616

Shakespeare dies.

1619

Richard Burbage, the great Elizabethan actor, and the first person ever to play Othello, dies.

1623

Anne Hathaway Shakespeare dies; the First Folio, a collection of Shakespeare's complete works, is published.

1745

Renowned English actor David Garrick plays Othello.

1785

English theater great John Philip Kemble earns acclaim for his portrayal of the Moor, at the time considered one of Shakespeare's two or three greatest characters.

1814

Another English actor, Edmund Kean, plays Othello to rave reviews.

1902

English actor Johnston Forbes-Robertson plays Othello at London's Lyric Theater.

1930

The American tour of Margaret Webster's then controversial production of *Othello,* starring American black actor Paul Robeson, is canceled because of fears of violent reaction by American audiences; a revival of the production, with José Ferrer playing Iago to Robeson's Othello, later opens on Broadway (in 1943) and runs for almost three hundred performances, then a record for a Shakespearean play in the United States.

1955

American actor-director Orson Welles releases his film version of *Othello,* with himself in the title role and Michael MacLiammòir in the part of Iago.

1964

Legendary English actor Laurence Olivier plays Othello in a production for England's recently formed National Theater, with Frank Finlay as Iago; some critics call Olivier's bravura performance a landmark in theater history; a year later the production is preserved on film, for which Olivier receives one of many Oscar nominations.

1982

American actor James Earl Jones plays Othello to English actor Christopher Plummer's Iago in a well-reviewed U.S. tour.

1995

American actor Laurence Fishburne plays Othello and English actor Kenneth Branagh Iago in a film of the play directed by Oliver Parker.

For Further Research

Text, Analysis, and Criticism of *Othello*

James L. Calderwood, *The Properties of* Othello. Amherst: University of Massachusetts Press, 1989.

Wim Coleman, ed., *Othello*. Logan, IA: Perfection Form Company, 1987.

John W. Draper, *The* Othello *of Shakespeare's Audience*. New York: Octagon Books, 1966.

E.A.J. Honigmann, ed., *Othello*. The Arden Shakespeare. Surrey, England: Thomas Nelson and Sons, 1997.

Alvin Kernan, ed., *Othello*. New York: New American Library, 1963.

Norman Sanders, ed., *Othello*. New York: Cambridge University Press, 1984.

Susan Snyder, *Othello: Critical Essays*. New York: Garland Publishing, 1988.

Elmer E. Stoll, *Othello: An Historical and Comparative Study*. New York: Gordion Press, 1967.

Virginia M. Vaughan, *Othello: A Contextual History*. New York: Cambridge University Press, 1994.

Alice Walker and John D. Wilson, eds., *Othello*. New York: Cambridge University Press, 1971.

Martin L. Wine, *Othello: Text and Performance*. London: Macmillan, 1984.

Louis B. Wright and Virginia A. LaMar, eds., *Othello*. New York: Simon and Schuster, 1967.

Shakespeare's Life and World

Gerald E. Bentley, *Shakespeare: A Biographical Handbook*. Westport, CT: Greenwood, 1986.

Marchette Chute, *Shakespeare of London*. New York: E.P. Dutton, 1949.

François Laroque, *The Age of Shakespeare.* New York: Harry N. Abrams, 1993.

———, *Shakespeare's Festive World: Elizabethan Seasonal Entertainment and the Professional Stage.* New York: Cambridge University Press, 1991.

Peter Levi, *The Life and Times of William Shakespeare.* New York: Henry Holt, 1989.

A.A. Mendilow and Alice Shalvi, *The World and Art of Shakespeare.* New York: Daniel Davey, 1967.

Peter Quennell, *Shakespeare: A Biography.* Cleveland: World, 1963.

A.L. Rowse, *Shakespeare: A Biography.* New York: Harper and Row, 1963.

———, *Shakespeare the Man.* New York: Harper and Row, 1973.

Samuel Schoenbaum, *William Shakespeare: A Compact Documentary Life.* New York: Oxford University Press, 1977.

STAGE PRODUCTIONS OF SHAKESPEARE'S PLAYS

John C. Adams, *The Globe Playhouse: Its Design and Equipment.* Cambridge, MA: Harvard University Press, 1942.

Sally Beauman, *The Royal Shakespeare Company: A History of Ten Decades.* Oxford: Oxford University Press, 1982.

John R. Brown, *William Shakespeare: Writing for Performance.* New York: St. Martin's Press, 1996.

Cecil De Banke, *Shakespeare Production, Then and Now.* London: Hutchinson, 1954.

Gordon Grosse, *Shakespearean Playgoing, 1890–1952.* London: Mowbray, 1953.

G.B. Harrison, *Elizabethan Plays and Players.* Ann Arbor: University of Michigan Press, 1956.

Robert Speaight, *Shakespeare on the Stage.* London: Collins, 1973.

Ronald Watkins, *On Producing Shakespeare.* New York: Benjamin Blom, 1964.

SHAKESPEAREAN ACTORS AND FILM ADAPTATIONS

Ivor Brown, *Shakespeare and the Actors.* New York: Coward McCann, 1970.

Anthony Davies and Stanley Wells, *Shakespeare and the Mov-*

ing Image: The Plays on Film and Television. Cambridge, England: Cambridge University Press, 1994.

Charles W. Eckert, *Focus on Shakespearean Films.* Englewood Cliffs, NJ: Prentice-Hall, 1972.

John Gielgud, *An Actor and His Times.* London: Sidgwick and Jackson, 1979.

Anthony Holden, *Laurence Olivier: A Biography.* New York: Atheneum, 1988.

Jack J. Jorgens, *Shakespeare on Film.* Bloomington: Indiana University Press, 1977.

Roger Manvell, *Shakespeare and the Film.* London: Debt, 1971.

Laurence Olivier, *On Acting.* New York: Simon and Schuster, 1986.

Richard L. Sterne, *John Gielgud Directs Richard Burton in Hamlet: A Journal of Rehearsals.* New York: Random House, 1967.

Peter Whitehead and Robin Bean, *Olivier: Shakespeare.* London: Lorrimer Films, 1966.

GENERAL GUIDES TO SHAKESPEARE'S PLAYS

Isaac Asimov, *Asimov's Guide to Shakespeare.* New York: Avenel Books, 1978.

Ronald Berman, *A Reader's Guide to Shakespeare's Plays: A Discursive Bibliography.* Glenview, IL: Scott, Foresman, 1973.

Charles Boyce, *Shakespeare: A to Z: The Essential Reference to His Plays, His Poems, His Life and Times, and More.* New York: Facts On File, 1990.

Marchette Chute, *Stories from Shakespeare.* New York: New American Library, 1956.

Norrie Epstein, *The Friendly Shakespeare: A Thoroughly Painless Guide to the Best of the Bard.* New York: Viking Penguin, 1993.

G. Blakemore Evans and J.J.M. Tobin, gen. eds., *The Riverside Shakespeare.* Boston: Houghton Mifflin, 1974.

Harley Granville-Barker and G.B. Harrison, eds., *A Companion to Shakespeare Studies.* Cambridge, England: Cambridge University Press, 1959.

Karl J. Holzknecht, *The Backgrounds of Shakespeare's Plays.* New York: American Book Company, 1950.

Charles and Mary Lamb, *Tales from Shakespeare.* New York: Macmillan, 1963.

Kenneth Muir and Samuel Schoenbaum, eds., *A New Companion to Shakespeare Studies.* Oxford: Oxford University Press, 1971.

GENERAL SHAKESPEAREAN ANALYSIS AND CRITICISM

Editor's Note: In addition to the works listed below, I highly recommend the many fine volumes in the series titled *Shakespeare Survey.* Published annually beginning in 1948 by Cambridge University Press, these books constitute a treasury of information about, commentary on, and criticism of Shakespeare's plays and various stage and film adaptations of these works.

Roy Batterhouse, ed., *Shakespeare's Christian Dimension: An Anthology of Commentary.* Bloomington: Indiana University Press, 1994.

A.C. Bradley, *Shakespearean Tragedy.* 1956. Reprint, New York: Viking Penguin, 1991.

Lily B. Campbell, *Shakespeare's Tragic Heroes: Slaves of Passion.* New York: Barnes and Noble, 1930, 1968.

Edmund K. Chambers, *William Shakespeare: A Study of Facts and Problems.* New York: Oxford University Press, 1989.

Cumberland Clark, *Shakespeare and the Supernatural.* London: Williams and Norgate, 1931.

William Empson, *Essays on Shakespeare.* New York: Cambridge University Press, 1986.

M.D. Faber, *The Design Within: Psychoanalytic Approaches to Shakespeare.* New York: Science House, 1970.

Brian Gibbons, *Shakespeare and Multiplicity.* Cambridge, England: Cambridge University Press, 1993.

Harley Granville-Barker, *Prefaces to Shakespeare.* 2 vols. Princeton, NJ: Princeton University Press, 1947.

Clifford Leech, ed., *Shakespeare: The Tragedies: A Collection of Critical Essays.* Chicago: University of Chicago Press, 1965.

Carolyn R.S. Lenz et al., eds., *The Woman's Part: Feminist Criticism of Shakespeare.* Urbana: University of Illinois Press, 1980.

Maynard Mack Jr., *Killing the King: Three Studies in Shakespeare's Tragic Structure.* New Haven, CT: Yale University Press, 1973.

Dieter Mehl, *Shakespeare's Tragedies: An Introduction.* New York: Cambridge University Press, 1986.

Don Nardo, ed., *Readings on* Hamlet. San Diego: Greenhaven Press, 1999.

——, *Readings on* Julius Caesar. San Diego: Greenhaven Press, 1999.

——, *Readings on* Romeo and Juliet. San Diego: Greenhaven Press, 1998.

Clarice Swisher, ed., *Readings on the Tragedies of William Shakespeare.* San Diego: Greenhaven Press, 1996.

Thomas F. Van Laan, *Role-Playing in Shakespeare.* Toronto: University of Toronto Press, 1978.

INDEX